# No Other God

*By the same author*

The Death of God

Wait Without Idols

# No Other God

Gabriel Vahanian

GEORGE BRAZILLER
New York

For information address the publisher:
*George Braziller, Inc.*
*One Park Avenue, New York 16, N.Y.*
Library of Congress Catalog Card Number: 66-28591
*First Printing*
Printed in the United States of America

For permission to quote from copyright material, grateful acknowledgment is made:

To Mr. Richard Wilbur for quotation from THE FLOWERS OF EVIL by Charles Baudelaire, edited by Jackson and Marthiel Matthews (New Directions).
To Mr. Jackson Matthews for quotation from THE FLOWERS OF EVIL by Charles Baudelaire, edited by Jackson and Marthiel Matthews (New Directions).
To Bollingen Foundation for quotation from WINDS by Saint-John Perse, translated by Hugh Chisholm (Pantheon).
To Grove Press, Inc. for quotation from WAITING FOR GODOT by Samuel Beckett.
To Harcourt, Brace and World, Inc. for quotation from THE ROCK by T. S. Eliot.
To Sheed and Ward, Inc., for quotation from CHRIST AND APOLLO by William F. Lynch, S.J., © Sheed & Ward, Inc., 1960.
To Meridian Books-World Publishing Company for quotation from EXISTENCE AND FAITH by Rudolf Bultmann, translated and selected by Schubert Ogden.

The scripture quotations in this book are from the Revised Standard Version of the Bible, copyright 1946–1952 by the Division of Christian Education, National Council of Churches, and are used by permission.

# Acknowledgments

The substance of "Calvin: Theology and the Death of God" was delivered in the form of a lecture at the Southern California School of Theology on 27 May 1964. Different parts of "The Word of God and the Word of Man" were read at the annual convention of the American Academy of Religion in Nashville (28 December 1965) and at the Third Consultation on Hermeneutics held at Drew University (22 April 1966). An earlier version of "No Other God" was used during the IXth Biennial Convocation at Princeton University (10 March 1966). "The End of the Age of Religion?" formed also the substance of an address delivered at Boston University (11 February 1966) and at Garrett Theological Seminary (13 May 1966). And I have translated and adapted the text of "The Church, the World, and Ethics" from an article based on an inquiry formulated by *Christianisme Social.*

"The Poverty of Theology" was first published in *The Christian Century* LXXXII, 49 (8 December 1965) under the title "Swallowed Up By Godlessness."

"The End of the Age of Religion?" was first published, without the notes, in the polyglot journal *Concilium* 16 (June 1966) and translated from the French by Mother Kathryn Sullivan, RSCJ, to whom I record here the expression of my sincere gratitude.

I wish to thank the editors of *The Christian Century* and *Concilium* for their permission to make use again of these materials.

G. V.

I am the Lord your God, who brought you out of Egypt, out of the house of bondage. You shall have no other gods before me. You shall not make yourself a graven image, or any likeness of anything that is in heaven above, or that is in the earth beneath, or that is in the water under the earth.

(Exod. 20/2–4)

. . . to whom shall we go? You have the words of eternal life.

(John 6/68)

# Contents

# Introduction

TAKEN AS NOTHING LESS IF NOTHING MORE THAN A CULTURAL phenomenon, the death of God signifies the transition from radical monotheism to radical immanentism and marks the birth of secularism as the vector of the new religiosity. More simply, it announces the advent of a new, culturally Christian, paganism, even while theology is busy overlooking its indigence or covering it up with a glorified but amnesic vocabulary. Indeed, accustomed to thinking of theology as an ecclesiastical task, as the self-critical task of the Church, we failed to realize that it had stopped speaking to the outside world and, *ipso facto,* to the Church itself, for the Church cannot understand itself unless the language of its self-understanding speaks to the world and unless the world itself can use the same language.

But what I have denounced elsewhere as the charter of an incipient post-Christian idolatry is now proclaimed as the first article of an immanentist religiosity. So-called "Christian atheism" glories precisely in what I deplored when I first used the term "death of God"; and it can do so, furthermore, only by appealing to the disaffected, though still residually Christian, religiosity of Western man. What I denounced, the "Christian atheists" now advocate, but only because they have in effect turned Sartre's definition of man as a useless passion into a soteriological program, not realizing that if godless man no longer needs God to understand himself, neither—as Sartre and Camus show—does he need God to establish himself as his own contradiction. I should have hoped that the "Christian atheists" would not lag so far behind real atheists, at a time when even these admit to the superannuated character of the conflict between theism and atheism.

Be that as it may, by restricting the role of theology to that of a watchdog over the tradition of the Church, God was being removed from the world. Theology served only to separate the Church from the world, instead of pointing to the fact that the Church is—or should be—what happens when the world hears the Word of God.

Theology is that critical and self-critical task of faith by which the world becomes the Church and the Church manifests the reality of the world. Whatever can be said against the older theology, one cannot take away from it the fact that it was spoken in the language of both the Church and the world. And what prevents theology from dissolving itself into religious, or ethical, or semantic immanentism is precisely what the tradition called, in the strict sense, *theo–logy*. Therein lies the radicalism of faith if by faith is meant the Christian faith and not any of its edulcorated substitutes.

The problem of God today is thus the primary problem of theology, not so much because that would be consonant with the tradition as because that is the only way of saying "no" to an idolatrous religiosity which would preserve of its heritage only its cultural aspects. It is easy to do away with theo–logy. How does one do away with idolatry? Nor is there any point in rejecting anthropomorphism only in order to rush headlong into anthropolatry, or Christosophy. Without God no Jesus: this is the corollary of the New Testament's without Jesus no God.

Equally important are both ecclesiology and ethics. To be a Christian does not mean to be a member of a community whose social and intellectual structures are antiquated. There is no city of God unless it assumes the city of man, and there is no Christian community unless it asserts the community of man. A Church which is one institution among others ceases to be *in* the world and becomes part *of* the world.

# The Poverty of Theology

Now on the first day of the week Mary Magdalene came to the tomb early, while it was still dark, and saw that the stone had been taken away from the tomb. So she ran, and went to Simon Peter and the other disciple, the one whom Jesus loved, and said to them, "They have taken the Lord out of the tomb, and we do not know where they have laid him."

(John 20/1–2)

# I

## The Poverty of Theology

It is evident that the death of God does not mean the same thing to all those who have proclaimed it.[1] From Jean Paul and Nietzsche to Jean-Paul Sartre and the "Christian atheists" one may also wonder, therefore, whether it is the same God who has been so loudly autopsied. Even so, none of this would be shocking if it were the prelude to a new religion or to pure and unadulterated godlessness. But our self-styled atheists today, whose system of thought could appropriately be termed "atheosophy" or, perhaps better, "Christosophy" (since they make it sound more positive than negative), also profess to be Christian.[2]

A contradiction in terms? No, if we listen to them and, with them, remember in particular that the early Christians themselves were charged with atheism. In fact, the new "Christian atheists" are so far from being able to see any contradiction between Christianity and their so-called atheistic Christosophy that one wonders on the one hand what has happened to the scandal and foolishness of the gospel and, on the other, whether this new step is not a part of the fatal acculturation in which Christianity has compromised itself but which these new atheists or Christosophists seem to denounce vehemently.

If the death of God has occurred—and indeed it has—it is not by capitulating to, or by coming to terms with, the resultant immanentist cultural frame of thought that Christianity is going to become relevant to our present situation, unless, of course, Christosophy is still fighting the old battle which was lost in the death of God. This is why the so-called Christosophical alternative to the fossil that Christianity has become—the flamboyant and fervent descriptions notwithstanding—either is merely the ultimate though opposite consecration of mystical rationalism or is the supreme though inverted rationalization of mystical deism.

Compound the absence or the remoteness of God as you will, this does not necessarily mean that the reality of godlessness will be accepted as a possible authentic alternative to Christianity. On the contrary, the result may be simply another self-explanatory system which, like all such systems, makes sense ultimately only by bypassing the truth it intended to expound, namely, that of the gospel which puts all our self-verifying truths into question. In order for such systems to stand, either God must be invented if he does not exist or he must be killed if he does. Both concepts are deficient because they are both predicated on SOMETHING which either is missing or is *de trop*. Certainly, we must correlate the gospel with the empirical, even atheistic, truths modern man lives by. But do we need to confuse them as well?

## 1

It was bad enough to inherit a God-based concept which had lost all concrete meaning. It is incomparably worse to attenuate and in fact deny the reality of the death of God by sublimating it into a newfangled soteriological concept. The death of God makes sense and is indeed a liberating event only when it is considered as a cultural phenomenon.

But to argue that a historical fact as such (perso prefer to call it a cultural phenomenon) totally and exclusively lays claim to my whole existence amounts to making it a new absolute, an idol hailed at the front door with all the red-carpet treatment while God is whisked out through the back door. Also, I do not see how, by turning a cultural event into an article of faith, such an attitude differs from the old *credo quia absurdum est.*

The Christian faith is radical only if it is iconoclastic; it is neither when it enraptures itself in the cult of the Golden Calf. Indeed, which position is more radical: simply to hold that the death of God is the cultural event that definitively seals the transition from the Christian to the post-Christian era, or to turn it into some necessary soteriological premise? Which is more iconoclastic: to recognize that godlessness is today a valid alternative to faith in God precisely because it denies not only God but any other kind of universal hypothesis—including itself—or to replace the old God-hypothesis with its converse, one distilled from the death of God? Granted, the early Christians were called atheists. But that was because, rejecting the cult of the emperor, they would not surrender to the religious syncretism to which their contemporaries were addicted. And though they all had the same worldview, the early Christians nonetheless considered the prevailing religious self-understanding of man as the sickness, not the remedy.

But the new Christosophy not only surrenders to the secularism of our time; it views this secularism as the remedy instead of the sickness. Not that Christianity must always systematically oppose the world and its wisdom. Rather, it cannot satisfy itself with them and rest in them if it must make them possible and honor them. That is why, in keeping with the gospel, I feel that the more secular theology is, the less it will be predicated on secularism, just as Saint Paul's theology was not predicated on the religious exigencies of his listeners in whose vernacular he proclaimed the gospel. All of us, incidentally, would do well to ponder the experience of those who undertook the task of translating the Latin mass into the vernacular only to discover that it became even less understandable.

## 2

Once again, which is more radical today: to let faith question and especially be itself questioned, or to be swallowed up by godlessness; to recognize that theology is vulnerable, or to erect it into a science unquestionably consistent with itself only because it has capitulated to the atheistic exigencies of a contemporary worldview?

As the cultural phenomenon which has alienated us both religiously and culturally from the Biblical conception of God, the death of God is what prevents us—much more effectively than any atheosophy or any sermon—from putting our trust in religion and its paraphernalia, or any substitute for them. Transformed into an article of faith, it becomes the springboard for a new religiosity. To put the gospel upside down or inside out results not in a religionless Christianity, much less in a godless Christianity, but in an ersatz which is not less religious for being godless. At least God-talk has the merit of having once been relevant. And I do not see how the secularism of the new religiosity is going to be successful precisely where religion itself has failed. If from the Biblical point of view it is not religion that saves, one can scarcely avoid realizing that it is not secularism, either.

The more one thinks about it the odder it seems that these new Christosophists, who began with the idea of a religionless Christianity, or its corollary, the secularization of Christianity, should end up with nothing more to offer than the same old opium. Meanwhile they remind us that despite their claims, Christianity, even if secularized and atheistic, remains what it has always also been—religion. But with this difference: Biblical Christianity represents that religious consciousness in which man is saved not by but in spite of, as well as from, his religiosity and its implicit positivism (which is what Feuerbach may have meant when he said that "atheism . . . is the secret of religion").

We must confess therefore that Bonhoeffer's proposal of a "religionless Christianity," though perhaps not ill-founded, has certainly been ill-construed, if not by him at least by those who have developed it into what is indeed its logical conclusion—a godless Christianity or, more exactly, a non-Christian religion. Feuerbach, when he reduced theology to mere anthropology, was at least more consistent than our Christosophists who eliminate all significance from the death of God and turn it into a hoax.

Indeed, to admit that the biblical worldview is no longer valid need not prevent our recognition that the reality of God was affirmed not because of but in spite of that worldview, however transcendental or sacral it was considered. Consequently, although the Bible was written in terms of a given worldview we can still claim that it neither has nor is a worldview in itself, and that consequently no worldview, immanentist or otherwise, *ipso facto* invalidates theology or faith in God. As a matter of fact, an immanentist worldview might yet help us to grasp and live more concretely the meaning of faith as eschatological existence: for the first time in twenty centuries God is not a crutch, God is not "reasons."

There is another factor muddling the sane approach to the significance of the death of God as a cultural phenomenon and ultimately denying its reality. This factor has two aspects. The first concerns the wailing over the realization that because of the secularization of Christianity we have lost the sense of the sacred and the world itself has lost its sacral dimension. The second is actually the converse of the first; it consists of the positivistic contention that the secular is the real and the real is the secular. What we are told in effect is that either Christianity makes sense only within the context of a certain worldview—a sacral one—or that Christianity cannot make sense today unless, in accordance with our contemporary atheistic worldview, we separate its original truth from the instrument that was once used to convey this truth.

## 3

These two seemingly contradictory aspects coalesce in the idea that, on the one hand, a sacral conception of the universe need not be theistic and, on the other, that "God" had nothing to do with the truth that was conveyed but was an element of or an adjunct to the vehicle of that truth and is therefore to be excised for the sake of preserving that truth. It may be so. But then we must be candid enough to admit either that this has nothing to do with the gospel or that we are back where we started from and it is time for us to recognize that the task is to write a new gospel, not to patch up the old one.

In offering an alternative to this dilemma, let us recognize that Christianity did not secularize, but desacralized, the world. Secularization is a symptom of another phenomenon; i.e., loss of faith or the betrayal of faith by the very institutions and creeds and dogmas meant to incarnate or transmit it. From the beginning faith had to desacralize the world or to dedivinize nature if it really meant (as Bultmann puts it) to "give back to the world its authentic worldliness." That in this process Christianity itself was secularized and gave birth to secularism is obviously another problem. Faith calls for secularity; secularism is the condition that dissolves faith and that results from the separation of the secular from the religious, of man's involvement in the world from his commitment to God. Because God is the creator and because his creation is not divine, the Bible holds that true secularity is the only religious mode of being; and by not separating the secular from the religious it also affirms, so to speak, that the secular is the real and the real is the religious. This is to say, the world is not divine but is the theater of God's glory, and true secularity is as different from secularism as it is from pantheism. The Church and its creeds and practices have become outmoded, but in the main they were once the means by which the secular was affirmed.

Let us conclude by saying that from the Biblical point of view the demarcation line is not between the sacred and the profane or between the religious and the secular—let alone between one worldview and another, or between theism and atheism (as I have tried to show in *Wait Without Idols*). The line is drawn between God and the idol, between the creator and the creature. It is drawn between iconoclasm and idolatry. No worldview—atheistic or theistic—can prevent either self-deification or God's becoming the idol from which man is constantly to be set free in order to become that which he is not, namely, himself rather than God.

# The End of the Age of Religion?

Today's atheism is tomorrow's religion.
(Feuerbach)

# The End of the Age of Religion?

[illegible]

# II

## The End of the Age of Religion?

Instead of looking at the world as the theater of God's glory, modern man is tempted to see the supernatural world of yesterday as the miserable theater, if not the theater-of-the-absurd misery, of man.

Whether this modern idea of the world be true or false, it is radically opposed to the world of the Bible and of the Christian tradition. The biblical worldview is transcendental, ours is immanentist. According to Bultmann's formula, the first is mythological, the second is scientific.[1] In the former, the here is meaningless apart from the hereafter; the contingent reality of the world presupposes the necessary reality of God. In the latter, the reality of God is no more than a hypothesis which modern science finds neither necessary nor useful; human existence has no other context than this world. Whereas the biblical vision of the world seems shot through with religiosity, our vision frankly wants to be secular and profane. That is why modern man in his desire to affirm both himself and the world cannot tolerate a Christianity that denies and negates the world. And, realizing his alienation from Christianity both religiously and culturally, more or less disillusioned, he reaches the conclusion that the age of religion has come to an end.[2]

## 1

It is not the first time that an age has come to an end. Did not the Judaeo-Christians of Antioch experience something comparable when the apostle Paul insisted that the gospel must be de-Judaicized in order both to preserve its integrity and make it accessible to pagans (Gal. 2/11–21)? In the flamboyant syncretism of the Graeco-Roman world, may we not conjecture that Paul's Judaeo-Christian questioners feared that he was running the risk of betraying and subjugating not merely Judaism but also Christianity to the idolatrous exigencies of a religiosity that actually denied the transcendence and the uniqueness of the God of Israel?

To be sure, the future would prove just the opposite, and the Christians were charged with atheism because they refused to worship the emperor. Nevertheless the important point was not so much the success of the operation but Paul's diagnosis: that it was in spite of religion as well as in spite of disbelief, however religious it might be, that the gospel must be proclaimed. At each successive stage a similar concern was felt at the decisive crossroads of Western Christianity. Is this true today?

The gulf that separates Christianity from the modern world is infinitely greater than the gap between nascent Christianity and the pre-Christian world. The fundamentally atheistic mentality of the present century seems to be totally alien to Christian premises. Should we therefore follow Saint Paul's example and, so to speak, "de-baptize" the gospel? This is the step that some seem to suggest in a desperate attempt to stem the growing lag between the traditional patterns of Christianity and modern thought. But the most radical step consists not in de-Chistianizing the faith but in retrieving Christianity both from occidentalism and from religiosity.

The first solution would reduce Christianity to one form of ideology among others, which would mean the negation of theology itself. The second, by contrast, would provide an opportunity of making the Christian faith contemporary without at the same time subordinating it to the immanentist exigencies of present-day anthropology.

Our task, to put it in another way, is much more complex than was that of Saint Paul. While the question he confronted was only a theological one, ours is at the same time both religious and cultural. More than a theological reformation, our task is to lay the foundations of an unprecedented reconversion of the *object* of theology (not of its *subject,* which is God) as well as of the structure of the Church and of its moral, social, political, and cultural action.

A visit to a few old villages quickly shows to what point the spiritual influence of the Church has depended on its geographical position, like the university in which theology through its object was the queen of all knowledge. Possibly this was relevant at a time when society was, if not static, at least stable. But in a mobile society like ours such a geographical and centripetal conception of the Church cannot dispel the haunting impression that, once a state within a state, the Church has become only a society within society, whose members may bow to one another but who do not speak.

The priest workers understood this. For them, as for Saint Paul, existing structures of society are meant to be the instruments for the spread of the gospel: indeed, the gospel need not stake its validity and actuality on the outdated structures of the Church. Because the Church is an eschatological reality and an article of faith (*Credo ecclesiam*) it must be careful not to perpetuate ecclesial forms that are due more to historical contingencies than to its spiritual vocation in the world. The Church should be on its guard lest it transform itself into an empirical datum whose sociological aspects and intellectual values serve only to confirm its attachment either to a past social order, or to a now naïve religious view of the world.[3] A Church that came out of its ghetto but still kept its old ways and mentality would succeed merely in turning its faith into an anachronism.

## 2

The transmission of the Christian faith has until now been predicated on categories that shared in a religious worldview. But today, by identifying itself with, while at the same time seeking to purify, such a worldview, and by accommodating itself to the resulting cultural structures, Christianity has intensified the double alienation, religious and cultural, which causes modern man to live his life under the sign of the death of God. As a phenomenon that is as much religious as cultural, the death of God ensures the transition from transcendence to immanence as determinative of the human experience and marks an awareness in which the superfluity of God—whether he is or not—is the predicate.

Even if scientific and technical empiricism may be said to have aided and partially justified such an evolution, Christianity itself is not to be exonerated. It was neutralized long ago, as a whole screen of dogmas or religious attitudes testify; vainly it was hoped that these would arrest the decline either by reducing Christianity to the essence of religiosity, or by making religiosity the essence of Christianity. But neither Catholic dogmatism nor Protestant scholasticism on the one hand, nor on the other the religious romanticism of Schleiermacher or Chateaubriand could succeed in preventing Kierkegaard and Nietzsche from unmasking and proclaiming the fraud; the former in diagnosing the demise of Christianity, the latter in crying: God is dead.

At the same time a new post-Christian civilization was in process of being born. Its universe was no longer made up of *vestigia Dei,* nor was God man's reason for being. More significantly, atheism ceased to be an intellectual imposture that was merely rhetorical so that it could become in its practical form the expression of a hypothesis of existence as valid as theism. The so-called religious experience having become *one* aspect of the total human experience, men discovered that the latter could be lived without the former.[4]

This does not mean that God is by definition excluded, but it does oblige us to recognize that the morality of the believer is not the guaranty but the test of the believer's faith (Job). Still less does it exclude the possibility that, in thus taking away from us all recourse to God as an epistemological or existential hypothesis, contemporary atheism has come to look at man almost as the Bible itself once did.[5] Hence, instead of rejecting atheism, we should seek to emphasize its contribution to the understanding of faith. Indeed, the man who lives under the sign of the death of God is not only the unbeliever but the unbeliever which I am despite my faith,[6] the only difference being that the significance the believer attributes to the work of Christ, the unbeliever discovers in avowing the death of God. It is this avowal that prevents him from seeing the fraud that he commits in seeking to establish his innocence, in which he can no more than capture the reflection of his own contradiction. However strange it may be, contemporary atheism is in fact an atheology of man without God.

## 3

This atheism was all the more inevitable because, although not necessary as the result of the desacralization of the world, it became necessary as soon as this desacralization could not be realized without the concomitant secularization of Christianity. The desacralization of the world—it is both wrong and pleonastic to speak of the secularization of the world—follows directly from the fundamental idea of creation: the world cannot be sacred because God alone, the creator, is holy.[7] Secularization, by way of contrast, describes the process through which Christianity has always tended to allow itself to be enclosed in its cultural and intellectual expressions and to be domesticated by them. Occidentalism is the higher form of this double phenomenon, secularism the lower form. If desacralization is one aspect of the action of Christianity on the world, secularization is one aspect of the action of the world on Christianity.

It is in and through the world that God's holiness manifests itself. It dwells in the world and, no matter whether the world be conceived as profane or religious, it is the world that constitutes the context where faith must assert its secularity[8] and the Church its eschatological reality: "Religion that is pure and undefiled before God and the Father is this: to visit orphans and widows in their affliction, and to keep oneself unstained from the world," like Abraham who, through faith, "sojourned in the land of promise, as in a foreign land (*tanquam in aliena*)" (James 1/27; Heb. 11/9; R.S.V.).

Faith understood as eschatological existence can no more withdraw from the world than devaluate the world; it gives the world its worldliness,[9] its secularity (John 17/15). By secularity I mean the attitude by which the Christian affirms faith as presence to the world at the same time that he affirms the original goodness of the world.[10] It is in being in the world that it is possible for the Christian to be not of the world. By contrast, secularism, which results from secularizing Christianity for the benefit of a world desacralized, fosters an attitude that is exactly the opposite of the *tanquam in aliena* of the epistle to the Hebrews.

In fact instead of preserving the utopian character (in the etymological sense of the word) of faith, in order "to keep oneself unstained from the world," history shows that Christianity has not always resisted the temptation to make it an empirical datum and, in so doing, has transformed it into religiosity . . . until the day when, like Laplace (who realized that he no longer needed any God-hypothesis on which to base his cosmology), men discovered that there is no empirical datum other than unbelief.

This explains why certain theologians, following Bonhoeffer, have advanced the idea of a non-religious Christianity. The better to grasp the fascinating and dangerous originality of this concept, we should first examine another aspect of the *malaise* that has seized Christianity.[11]

## 4

While from the sacral point of view the universe tends to transform itself into a kind of divine hypostasis, the Bible considers that God does not cease to be totally Other in relation to the world of which he is the creator, and in which he yet reveals his presence. This divine presence in the world is not mediated by a variety of *vestigia Dei,* but is manifested by his acts. The sacral conception gives primacy to nature over history. It is an-historical, if not anti-historical, while the Bible offers us an historical and sacramental conception of the world and the human reality (Gen. 28/10–22; Exod. 4/1–17). To say that this conception is sacramental means in particular that the world in itself is not able to attest the presence of God but can only do so charismatically, in spite of itself (Gen. 28/16 f.).

The sacral world is hostile to man. The sacramental world depends on man and offers itself to him as the theater of his activity, even while reminding him of his finitude. If, therefore, although bound to desacralize the world, early Christianity advocated a systematic refusal of the world instead of affirming it, this may have been because the charismatic quality of the creation's sacramental power had not been aptly taken into account. Later Catholicism was also to underestimate this charismatic quality of the world when it structured the meaning of the reality of the sacrament according to the categories of the sacred, while at the same time it transferred the sacred from the realm of nature to that of history and bestowed it on social, political, and ecclesiastic institutions of the Middle Ages.[12] As for Protestantism, if it understood holiness as belonging only to God, it did not always recognize that because of this very holiness of God and his grace, the world had not lost its sacramental power but had been invested with it all the more significantly, because it was not a right but a gift, a grace.

That is why medieval sacramentalism and Protestant spiritualism, even if they are otherwise biblically oriented, both represent a deviation from the biblical understanding of the charismatic value of the sacramental world. By different paths they both seek, either to make the faith a natural possibility for man, as if there were no discontinuity between the sinner and the justified man, or to make it the principle of a moral progressivism which ultimately can only lead to some sort of sociological segregationism.[13]

Opposed to this is Bonhoeffer's thought. Accepted by so many disciples, it easily presents itself with the trumps needed to convince us. Indeed, if the sacralist tendency represents in general the surnaturalist deviation of Catholicism, and the spiritualizing tendency represents the moralizing deviation of Protestantism, both nevertheless attain the same result: Christian life is viewed as based on the idea of a separation from the world[14] rather than of an action that manifests its eschatological vocation within the world through the very socio-cultural structures *of* the present world. Today more than ever the structures of the Church should exist only to enable it to function within or, rather, *through* the structures of the world and not vice versa.

On the other hand, the Christian's freedom justifies the responsibility he must assume toward the world. The Christian's commitment to God should be matched by a reciprocal involvement in the world. Otherwise faith runs the risk of becoming sacral or spiritual religiosity (Col. 2/16–23), while the world is surrendered to the profane, to the *saeculum,* to secularism which is today underwriting the failure of both sacralism and spiritualism as the solution of the problem.[15] This solution is proposed as consisting in a secularized and religionless Christianity.

## 5

In spite of the valid and even seductive intuition of the Bonhoeffer program, it is nonetheless true that his proposal of a religionless Christianity merits as many reservations as eulogies. The drama of Bonhoeffer's thought, anchored as it is in the conviction of the insurmountable incompatibility between faith and religion, is to succeed only in substituting a new dichotomy, that of atheism and theism, for the traditional cleavage between the sacred and the profane or the religious and the secular, and in laying the foundations for an innerworldly millenarianism instead of the otherworldly and transcendental millenarianism that Christian traditionalism based on the dyad of this world and the next.

The error is to continue to consider the problem of faith under the aspect of an antinomy, that of the Church and men or that of God and the world,[16] in which the roles are reversed: it is not the wretched sinner who stands before the majesty of God, it is man in all his strength who stumbles against the weakness of God.[17] That this means the abandonment of all claims to triumphalism can be willingly admitted, but what is the need of replacing triumphalism with a kenotic Christianity?

One must render to atheism what is its due, just as to Caesar what is Caesar's, and recognize with Bonhoeffer that to try to explain God's power by man's weakness is deliberate self-deception. But to draw the conclusion that the Christian must therefore live without God among men who are without God, as if God did not exist,[18] amounts to shifting Anselm's *etsi Deus non daretur* from the domain of logic to the domain of faith before proffering it as the ultimate object of an act of faith. It is obvious that in the twentieth century, more than ever before, humility becomes a Christian better than arrogance. But to explain the power of the "world come of age" by the powerlessness of God, when we should rather explain the attraction of atheism by the inconsistency of Christianity, is equivalent to attributing to God the weakness of the Christian.

It is evident that Christianity should not attribute to itself any religious or cultural particularism. That we should be atheists with atheists, as Paul made himself a Jew with Jews, certainly is in accordance with the freedom which the Christian enjoys in regard to all men *for the sake of God.* This is a question of human relations based on the conviction that faith can never serve as justification for any social segregation. But to define the Christian as a man whom God has abandoned and to make the world the theater of the absence of God or a domain whence God has withdrawn does not so much lead to a religionless Christianity as to the *mystique* of a faith whose axis is the dialectic of a God who is with us in the measure that we are without him.[19]

Bonhoeffer, like Paul (I Cor. 9/19–23), wishes to make himself all things to all men. But unlike Paul who wished to do this for the sake of God, Bonhoeffer wishes to do this *in spite of God.* The distinction is not unimportant. It indicates the transposition of the problem from one level to another, from that of existence to that of a speculation about the faith, from eschatology to a *mystique* of immanentism. Bonhoeffer rejects the old sociological distinction between the believer and the unbeliever, only to pick it up again in another domain, the domain of faith, where it does not belong. For faith is not composed of the *juxtaposition* of belief and unbelief. It merely affirms that unbelief waits in ambush for the believer as much as it blinds the unbeliever. Faith is not what can separate them. Nor can it affirm itself by denying itself.[20] The line of demarcation does not pass between believer and unbeliever, it passes between God and man. This is what Saint Paul suggests and the Apocalypse clearly asserts: "Let the evildoer still do evil, and the filthy still be filthy, and the righteous still do right, and the holy still be holy. Behold I am coming soon" (Apoc. 22/11–12; cf. Matt. 25/31–46). He who is and who was, Emmanuel, is the God who is coming.

## 6

Let us conclude with two remarks. First, if for the Bible the profane is just as real as the religious, the real, is the *eschaton.*[21] In other words, non-religion is an eschatological reality, it is not an empirical datum of the sociological or historical order. Secondly, whether he be religious or not, man always tends towards idolatry. So true is this that he would invent God if God did not exist or if he did exist man would kill him in order to legitimatize either the idolatry to which the ambiguities of existence subject him or the ambiguities into which idolatry plunges him.

Did not Saint Thomas himself say this when he spoke of the imperfect knowledge which is the natural knowledge of God?[22] Calvin also was quick to point out what a source of idolatry and superstition was the idea of God that flowered from "this seed of religion sown in all men."[23] As for Barth, while making Calvin's doctrine his own, it is Saint Thomas whom he approaches when he does not oppose religion to unbelief but to revelation which he defines as the abolition and *assumptio* of religion, religion being the highest expression of unbelief.[24] Was Feuerbach, therefore, right when he said that atheism was the secret of every religion?[25] Or was he wrong in not seeing that religion is the secret of all atheism?

To sum up: if it is true that the gospel could have been proclaimed thanks to a religious conception of the world to which Christianity in the end abdicated, is it not also a little bit in spite of this conception that in the time of the Apostles and since then this gospel was proclaimed? It is in spite of atheism that today this same gospel must be thought and believed and lived. But might it not be thanks, too, to the human and spiritual values that atheism also contains? It is not these values that faith should fear,[26] but the caricature of Christianity, its "simulacre," as they used to say in the past in referring to superstition and idolatry.

# No Other God

"You are my witnesses," says the Lord,
"and my servants whom I have chosen.
that you may know and believe me
and understand that I am He.
Before me no god was formed,
nor shall there be any after me.
I, I am the Lord,
and beside me there is no savior.
I declared and saved and proclaimed,
when there was no strange god among you;
and you are my witnesses," says the Lord.
"I am God, and also henceforth I am He;
there is none who can deliver from my hand;
I work and who can hinder it?"

(Isa. 43/10–13)

# III

## No Other God

As CHRISTIANITY'S BEQUEST TO MODERN MAN, THE DEATH OF God represents that cultural phenomenon in terms of which a transmutation in the historical texture of our existence makes it impossible for us, from where we stand, to go back to Jesus.

Without God, all that's left is Jesus, a historical figure whose life and work, although it could perhaps be regarded as the life and work of a "man for others," does not adequately account for what the tradition confessed in proclaiming him as the Christ, namely, that in and through this historical figure the God who can reveal himself is only the God who is "God for man." That this binds the reality of God to that of man need not be contested. It also signifies that the human reality is not exhausted by the contingencies of history, any more than it is by the caprices of nature. "If I do not believe in God," Feuerbach argues, "there is no God for me."[1] From a Christian point of view, it would be more appropriate to say: If I do not believe in God, there is no Christ for me; and Jesus becomes a mere historical character, sad and glorious, fierce but impotent, an epitaph of the human consciousness. Indeed, an evanescent Christology can only expose an obsolescent Christianity.

## 1

"God by himself is not God," writes Barth in *The Word of God and the Word of Man,* "He might be something else. Only the God who reveals himself is God."[2] By himself Jesus is not Christ. Nor, in this connection, is the structure of the Apostles' Creed without significance: Christology forms only the second article, not the first, even though, as the New Testament holds, one must believe in Jesus Christ in order to believe in God. The Christ-event brings to an end man's imaginations about God: "The true light that enlightens every man was coming into the world. He was in the world, and the world was made through him, yet the world knew him not" (John 1/9–11).

Indeed, in the Christ-event God conceals, even forsakes, his divinity. That is, he does not act as a god should according to man's imagination. He does not die; but the Christ-event signifies that the debilities and limitations of the human condition can become the arena of faith, "the victory that overcomes the world" (I John 5/4). Ever since Caesarea of Philippi, if it is not possible to say God without Christ, neither is it possible to confess Christ without God: "Now when Jesus came into the district of Caesarea Philippi, he asked his disciples, 'Who do men say that the Son of man is?' And they said, 'Some say John the Baptist, others say Elijah, and others Jeremiah or one of the prophets.' He said to them, 'But who do you say that I am?' Simon Peter replied, 'You are the Christ, the Son of the living God!' And Jesus answered him, 'Blessed are you, Simon Bar-Jona! for flesh and blood has not revealed this to you, but my Father who is in heaven'" (Matt. 16/13–17).

As flesh and blood alone Jesus is only an ideal man, scarcely the symbol of authority, much less that of faith

(Matt. 21/23–27). And in spite of Peter's denials and the cowardice of the other disciples, the story of the passion shows precisely how hopelessly they were committed to Jesus as flesh and blood. Had they not previously idolized Jesus, perhaps they would not have felt forsaken. Indeed all our gods are idols, and above all the god that dies.[3] "Why do you call me good? No one is good but God alone" (Luke 19/18).

Without God, Jesus becomes at best an idol, and ceases to be a man as the title Christ itself implies, or as the early Christological definitions painfully attempted to bring to light, so that not even the attribution of divinity to Christ circumvented his human condition as Jesus. Do we not misunderstand the Fathers of the Church when we fail to realize that a good deal of their talk about the divinity of Christ had to do with the "humanity" of God? Theology, as Vinet says,[4] has more often than not dealt with the tendency to diminish Deity rather than humanity. When all is said and done, one might yet come to the view that on the whole theology has not been concerned so much with a cold speculative concept of God as with the concrete human context in terms of which not only could God be believed in, but without which he could not be believed in. When Isaiah says, "I, I am the Lord and beside me there is no savior. I declared and saved and proclaimed, when there was no strange god among you; and you are my witnesses" (Isa. 43/11–12), Rabbi Simon Bar-Yochai interprets this in the following way: "If you are my witnesses I am God, and if you are not my witnesses I am, so to speak, no longer God."[5]

If there are no witnesses, then there is no God. Or as Paul puts it after listing all the witnesses to the risen Christ: "If the dead are not raised, then Christ has not been raised. If Christ has not been raised your faith is futile . . ." (I Cor. 15/16–17). The Christ-event, rather than culminating in the death of God, thus implies exactly the opposite: the reality of "the living God," as Peter puts it. And in the cross, it is not God who is being edged out of the world, as Bonhoeffer contends,[6] but our idols. For "there is no other name under heaven given among men by which we must be saved" (Acts 4/12).

Thus, rather than opening the way to Jesus, the death of God obstructs it, hermetically. If there are no witnesses to God, then "Christ has not been raised" and "faith is in vain" (I Cor. 15/14), and Jesus is a miscarriage of history. Rather than liberating Jesus from mythological and supernatural fetters, the death of God delivers him up to historical anonymity and alienates him from us, irretrievably.

## 2

Furthermore, if it is clear that the traditional self-understanding of man was predicated on the reality of God, it is equally clear that man could not grasp this reality of God without understanding himself, at the same time, as a man of a given situation. Because of the death of God, traditional Christianity precludes itself from enabling modern man to understand himself in any similar way, supposing that, in the first place, he was not blocked from it by his own religious and cultural alienation.

Of paramount importance is likewise the fact that the Christian understanding of God and man was postulated on the assumption of the religious nature of man, on the irreducibility of the human reality. Contrary to Bonhoeffer, the emergence of methodological atheism does not mean that we are moving toward an age of no religion at all,[7] but that the historical consciousness of Western man has undergone such a transmutation that the traditional understanding of religiosity as a special province of being has gone through a process of obliteration. But the result will be, if indeed it is not yet, a new characterization of man as *homo religiosus*. "Today's atheism," to quote Feuerbach again, who so discerningly wrote over a century ago even though from a slightly different perspective, "is tomorrow's religion."[8] The point I am making simply consists in the contention, or rather in the fact, that man's fundamental religiosity, though it brings forth empirically observable phenomena such as magic or rituals, is not ultimately reducible to any one of them. Not only, as Cassirer holds, *religio una est in varietate rituum,*[9] but in any kind of analysis of the human experience religiosity is what in the last resort prevents any type of reductionism, be it psychological or scientific, physiological or anthropological. Just as religion makes history irreversible, so also religiosity makes the human reality irreducible.

In saying this, I should not want to be suspected of advocating religion for the sake of religion. I am simply saying that man is a religious animal and that this fundamental religiosity need not, in order to be recognized, express itself according to the canons of any of the traditional historical religions. As a matter of fact, it is because this already is the case today that the modern worldview is in conflict with the classic mythological one, and undermines the secular relevance of the Christian faith. Here is also the reason for contending that if traditional Christianity is of no avail to man in the scientific age, he cannot, with the exception of those who still live off the traditional expressions of religiosity though on a different diet, find much help in the non-Western religions if only because these, too, belong in the same category of phenomenological consciousness as does the Christian religion. If the latter is obsolete, it is a safe thing to say that the former are bound to the same fate and that, moreover, post-Christian man is immune to them perhaps even more than to his own religious past.

Thus, the emergence of radical immanentism does not mean that man has today become less religious or non-religious. It may simply mean that Christianity, after conquering the paganism of antiquity, has in turn bred its own paganism, in the various secularistic creeds that have sequestrated traditional Christianity and neutralized it as a cultural, political, philosophical, i.e., theological ferment.

This vulnerability of the Christian faith hinges today on the fact that there can be no faith in God which does not assume a concomitant cultural obligation. There can be no faith without secularity. But without God there can only be secularism, whether or not it masquerades as religion. Should, then, the Christian faith be unable to overcome its present cultural estrangement brought about by the death of God, its only alternative is to become an esoteric mystery cult, that is, the very antithesis of what it has claimed to be for twenty centuries. It will increasingly become a private religion, whether on an individual and domestic basis or whether on the basis of a spiritually segregated collective experience such as the Church affords today in the suburbs of life. And the trouble with this sort of eventuality is that most Christians do not have the stamina of the Amish. As Vinet says: "To believe in God and find oneself unable to draw from it any practical consequences is, if you will, to believe in God; it also is, however, to be without God."[10]

Therefore, just as from the biblical point of view without witnesses there is no God, so also without a cultural vocation there can be, insofar as Christianity is concerned, no faith in God. And "faith apart from works is dead" (James 2/26).

## 3

I have said that if, for the New Testament, one must believe in Christ if one wants to believe in God, the problem we are faced with today is that without God we have no access to Jesus. I have also said that without witnesses and their works (i.e., man's given historical situation, his involvement in his world as an expression of his commitment to God) there is no God, at least none of whom the Christ-event is the empirical reality. Put differently this means that in order to speak about God one must speak about man. To do so, however, one must ultimately speak about Jesus Christ—that is to say, about God: exactly for this reason, however, nothing valid is said about Jesus (and, consequently, about God) if what is said overlooks the fact that Jesus was a man. The Johannine idea of the word become flesh stresses this fact as does Paul's Christological hymn of Philippians 2, not to mention the gospel passages where Jesus acts like a human being.

In biblical thought human existence is viewed both as nature and as history, as flesh and as spirit, as an empirical, physiological, or biological datum and as spiritual or eschatological reality, meaning thereby that man as spirit coincides with, and is identified *as* but not *with*, man as nature.

Man is created in the image of God. That this image is not a natural quality of man is evidenced by, or brings to light, the fact that even *qua* nature, let alone *qua* history, human existence is other than the sum total of its contradictions and achievements. And when one considers man *qua* history, it becomes all the more clear that this image is not so much a physical likeness as the verifying or authenticating act by which eschatological existence does not shun but assumes empirical existence in its totality. Indeed, man is created in the image of God only in the sense that God remains imageless.

Even in and through Christ, God remains imageless: Jesus is not a God, and Christ as God's empirical reality is so only from the standpoint of faith. And if Jesus said that "I and the Father are one" he did not, as Paul declares, "think to snatch at equality with God, but made himself nothing, assuming the nature of a slave. Bearing the human likeness, revealed in human shape, he humbled himself, and in obedience accepted even death—death on a cross." (Phil. 2/6–8.)

From this we learn two things:

1) The human nature of Jesus is not the appearance of some divine nature; the divine nature manifests itself in no other way than through the human nature. This is the same as saying that in Christ the word became flesh. This also means, however, that the human is the only access to the

divine. To be human is to have access to the divine or, rather, to be accessible to the divine. Even death does not preclude that, much less the death of God if one does not hypostasize it into an article of "faith."

2) Jesus is not some kind of substitute for God. Not only the traditional doctrine of the two natures but also that of the Trinity stakes the otherness of God on man's being such that eschatological existence does not remove him from the arena of natural existence. Otherwise, faith in God would become belief that God is this or that, here or there, a thing, an object—a god that dies. This precisely is the meaning of the Trinity and, in particular, of the procession of the Spirit from both the Father and the Son. The Trinity thus ceases to be a concept or, at least, a glorified metaphor, and becomes the expression of the plain fact that no man can believe in God except in a given concrete situation and that faith in God is no faith at all if man's concrete situation is thereby obliterated. Indeed, faith is the price man must pay if he thus wants to assume his contingency.

It becomes quite clear at this point that from the point of view of the tradition, the doctrine of the Trinity itself was not some kind of esoteric description of the nature of God *per se* but the theonomous and iconoclastic expression of the conviction that eschatological existence must body forth into historical existence. The Trinity, so to speak, was no short-cut to God through the deification of the man Jesus—much less was it, therefore, a short-cut to Jesus. This amounts to saying that one cannot talk about Jesus without first talking about God. Nor can one do this without being asserted at the same time as a man of a given situation.

On this basis, any speech about God is also an iconoclastic speech about man, about his secularism as well as his religiosity. Indeed, human speech itself calls for just that iconoclastic understanding of the human experience.

# The Word of God and The Word of Man

Aut quid dicit aliquis, cum de te dicit? Et vae tacentibus de te; quoniam loquaces muti sunt.

(Augustine)

# IV

## The Word of God and The Word of Man

WHILE NO WORD IS SACRAMENTAL EXCEPT CHARISMATICALLY, what gives meaning to a word is its sacramental power. A word has this sacramental power when an ultimately irreducible reality is spoken of in terms of a measurable empirical phenomenon. For example, to say that "all flesh is grass," whatever it may signify, establishes an analogy that prevents reducing the human reality to mere flesh, to a measurable quantity. That such a view confirms a certain similarity between what has traditionally been designated as a metaphoric word and what we here call a sacramental word, cannot be denied. But, while a metaphoric word merely determines a relation between measurable phenomena, either subjectively or objectively, by means of a mutual appropriation of their qualities, a sacramental word speaks of what ultimately makes these phenomena and their realities inalienable as well as irreducible. And because such phenomena may be viewed, at least according to biblical thought, as empirically unable to exclude the divine without simultaneously diminishing the human, any more than they can stifle the verbal nature of reality, man's word is truly sacramental when it is charismatically assumed by the Word of God. In this sense, the word of man is a sacrament of the Word of God.

Indeed, if it is true that even through the Christ-event God can be encountered only insofar as in man the spirit is asserted as flesh and the flesh is assumed by the spirit, then it follows that not even in the Bible can the Word of God be heard if it does not coincide with the word of man, if it does not establish the word of man.

Already in the New Testament, Herbert Braun observes, "Christian and also profane quotations take the place of the Torah."[1] Nothing is sacred about Scripture in itself, not even when it claims to be the repository of some divine revelation. As a matter of fact, insofar as Christianity is concerned, the concept of a sacred Scripture can only lead to a contradiction in terms unless it is understood to be a metaphor expressing the conviction that "the world of fact is a hieroglyphic of the Spirit."[2] Calvin himself likened the Bible to a pair of glasses man needs to wear if he wants correctly to decipher the text of the universe.[3] Every word, however profane and secular it may seem, performs a similar function simply by virtue of its being a human word. It may lead to God,[4] or it may not, as the nominalists of the late Middle Ages would have contended; unless, of course, in conformity with today's methodological atheism, one would rather state that the word of man is what should lead to God but does not, because the Word of God is not a natural determination of the word of man.

Though the Word of God and the word of man may coincide, the former "never becomes so incarnate in the word of man that they are one and the same."[5] The Word of God is the expression for the phenomenon of being able to speak the word of man,[6] which word cannot establish itself and may not do so without either eliminating the Word of God or simply contradicting the very nature of the word,[7] or, what amounts to the same thing, without violating the infinite qualitative difference between God and man.[8]

Even the closing of the biblical canon does not mean that God has stopped speaking. It means that, if the words of the biblical authors could be assumed by the Word of God, the word of man—any word, whether or not it shared in the worldview of Scripture—was now a phenomenon through which the Word of God could be heard.[9] As a matter of fact, in spite of appearances, traditional exegesis has at least been consistent with itself if only to the extent that it has rested on such a hermeneutic principle. In his scholarly treatment of medieval exegesis, Henri de Lubac shows how, in accordance with Origen and Augustine, it was constantly affirmed that the more one was versed in secular letters, the more penetratingly one could read divine Scripture, and the more understandably one could interpret it. Sacred Scripture shines and makes sense only through the secular disciplines, as Werner of Saint Blaise, among others, contended.[10]

Nor is the point of our argument to be construed as implying that the choice, so to speak, is between the Bible and secular literature. As Calvin argued, the authority of Scripture neither grounds itself in any theory of verbal inspiration nor depends on the authority of the Church.[11] "The necessity for Holy Scripture is not absolute" as Heppe seems to infer;[12] the authority of the Bible is but a *phenomenon of faith*. Indeed, from an empirical point of view, even the God to whom the Bible bears witness is only the *deus absconditus*, which is another way of saying that, as culturally determined human word, the Bible is no more than secular literature to be identified with the Word of God. To this aspect of the problem the Catholic tradition has rather consistently testified throughout the centuries by constantly advocating, at least for practical purposes, the primacy of the Church over Scripture. What, on the other hand, the Protestant tradition shows by making the authority of the Church dependent upon that of Scripture, is precisely the verbal nature of reality, including the human reality.

Through the word, the Word of God becomes a phenomenon of the world, as was Jesus himself *qua* historical figure. Consequently, nothing is more contrary to the spirit of the gospel than the idolization of Jesus or of the Bible, and it follows that the Word of God will not be heard through the word of man, except where the latter is established, nor Jesus become the Christ except where man is also asserted through that act of faith by which alone he can legitimately assume his contingency. What the Greeks called nature becomes here the domain of faith. And what they considered to be reason or the sense of proportion becomes here that iconoclastic quality of faith by which man assuming his contingency can improvise his destiny.

Whether spiritual or secular, the word of man hence constitutes a parable of his transcendental nature: not even his works can reduce him to a cultural or religious particularism. On the other hand, because "every civilization and every culture is thus a tower of Babel,"[13] man can never speak the last, the ultimate word, any more than he can be defeated by the unessential vacuity of his words or of his works: such is, as an empirical phenomenon, the meaning of Pentecost, of the Word of God. Nor does this seem so far fetched if one reflects on it as a consequence of the biblical view of the "humanity" of God. To put it crudely, the Bible speaks of the transcendence of God almost always as though it were an "empirical" phenomenon. Is this not, in fact, also the meaning of the New Testament's insistence on the necessity of Jesus Christ for God's accessibility to man? The word of man is man's access to the Word of God: no man can speak it, nor does any man speak who does not speak the Word.

## 1

In a short essay of July 1913, Alain writes: "All ideas have the same fate as the idea of God; they often obstruct the way they should open."[14] In another essay of the same year he states: "The God-thing, God in the inertia of his perfections, is what kills and will kill every religion. The Baal, the Golden Calf, the true God, it scarcely matters who, as soon as a statue is worshipped."[15] No wonder then, Alain argues, ultimately it is religion itself which is the condemnation of religion.[16] Leaving aside the question whether similarly literature, too, finally contradicts itself and, like religion, becomes its own condemnation, it will suffice simply to stress here the ultimate impotence of literature and its vanity, its "uselessness." The last word is Baudelaire's, who wrote in *The Albatross:*

> The poet is like this monarch of all the clouds,
> Familiar of storms, of stars, and of all high things;
> Exiled on earth amidst its hooting crowds,
> He cannot walk, borne down by his giant wings.[17]

Perhaps more appropriate to our argument is the declaration Baudelaire makes in one of his drafts for a preface to *The Flowers of Evil:*

> I had intended, at first, to answer numerous criticisms and at the same time to explain a few quite simple questions that have been totally obscured by modern enlightenment: What is poetry? What is its aim? On the distinction between the Good and the Beautiful; on the Beauty in Evil; . . . but this morning I was so rash as to read some of the public newspapers; suddenly an indolence of the weight of twenty atmospheres fell upon me, and I was stopped, faced by the appalling uselessness of explaining anything whatever to anyone whatever. Those who know can divine me, and for those who can not or will not understand, it would be fruitless to pile up explanations.[18]

In citing these references, all that is suggested is the idea that, in the universal process of civilizations, both religion and literature may be said—in spite of their distortions, their failures, even their meretricious tendencies—to be what ultimately opposes, loudly or faintly, the question mark against all the achievements, material as well as spiritual, by which a given culture deceives itself into its own ethnolatrous counterfeit, and religion into an acculturated phenomenon. In other terms, although literature and religion may vary in their respective purposes, they both are, at bottom, an attempt to formulate the image of an imageless reality, i.e., the verbal and ultimately irreducible nature of the human reality; and this explains why, when this aspect is neglected or violated, existence is encumbered either with clichés and slogans or with dogmatism and superstition.

Expressive of the verbal nature of the human reality, literature and religion alike, or any similarly imaginative or metaphoric function, will always question man's deed, and will question it as long as word and deed do not coincide. And as long as word and deed do not coincide, man will always be able at least to speak this word and thus to manifest his resistance to every form of objectification, whether religious or secular. Doubtless, man is what he does—or, for that matter, what he eats—but he is also defined by something more, something else: call it the weakness of his strength or the greatness of his misery, it is what I call a "word," that of religion, of literature, of art, even the word of any deed high or base that speaks louder than words; the word in, with and under our words, the word which awaits its meaning from our words because it gives them their meaning.

But what is a word? And what does it do?

## 2

It is no accident that as a sign the word means what it signifies only in an arbitary way. This is not because the ideal always denounces the shortcomings of the real, or because the real always belies the ideal. It is because the *real* always transcends and puts into question our realizations. I do not simply mean that an actual table is only an approximation of table-ness, or that there is incongruity between the word and what it names; I mean that the inadequacy of the word to what it names is not only a negative but also a positive factor. More precisely this inadequacy is at once negative and positive, and actually points to the fact that the word is an icon, the image of an imageless reality, which it can equally reveal and conceal, the way to which it can open or obstruct. (The iconostasis in a Greek Orthodox church is indeed what separates the holy of holies from the rest of the sanctuary.) But the word can open or obstruct the way only if it is *iconoclastic*—if it rebels against freezing reality into an image, a cliché, a slogan, or a dogma—even to the point where the word can partially if desperately recover its iconoclastic function only by sinking into a nihilistic, ultimate refusal of meaning, quite beyond the simple refusal to consider meaning as inherent in the thing which is named.

Anchored in the verbal nature itself of reality, the iconoclastic function of the word forces us to draw here a deceptively simple inference: the meaning of a table does not reside in the table. This is true even for onomatopoeic words. Nor does the meaning of the world reside in the world. In itself the world is meaningless: which is why it can be seen as the theater of God's glory. It has no purpose: which is why one speaks of God's continuous care of the world. It has no reality until it is created *ex nihilo* and sustained by the Word of God. What can the world possibly look like to man under such conditions? Is this not the question raised by that apparently meaningless juxtaposition of words Lucky spouts forth in Beckett's *Waiting for Godot* before physical muteness at last puts an end to his incoherent babble:

> LUCKY: Given the existence as uttered forth in the public
> works of Puncher and Wattman of a personal
> God quaquaquaqua with white bear
> quaquaquaqua outside time without extension
> who from the heights of divine apthia divine
> athambia divine aphasia loves us dearly with

some exceptions for reasons unknown but time
will tell and suffers like the divine Miranda with
those who for reasons unknown but time will tell
are plunged in torment plunged in fire whose fire
flames if that continues and who can doubt it will
for the firmament that is to say blast hell to heaven
so blue still and calm. . . .[19]

But the iconoclastic function of the word does not merely consist in the refusal of meaning; it also consists in the acceptance of meaning, in the assent to the meaningfulness of the word and, furthermore, in the assent to the reality of the world, a reality which eludes or even threatens man, but also awaits its realization from the hand of man by providing a context for the human experience. The world is "the sphere of man's action," of man's speech. It always stands in need of the word of man. It is man who gives meaning to the groaning of the creation and thus affirms its reality by acquiescing to it, while at the same time he transfigures it. It is in this sense that I understand the Genesis passage (2/19–20) where Adam names the animals. By naming them he does not acquire absolute control over them, but indicates that he is not controlled by them, even though the naming of a thing may be the first step toward its domestication rather than, as is the case here, a step toward the foundation of man as work, as history.

Constituting man as history, the word is the agent which in the last analysis forbids or frustrates the identification of man with his works, in order to transcend, even in a last breath, their ultimate incapacity to signify anything. Indeed, to name a thing means to transcend it; and to speak is to be irreducible to, though simultaneously inalienable from, any aspect, however humble and frail, of the human experience. Which amounts to saying that man's autonomy is no empirical datum and, accordingly, need not *ipso facto* exclude its being grounded in God. And that is why the name of God—who reveals his name and conceals it at the same time—is not pronounced in the Old Testament, in contrast with the New Testament where the name of Jesus stands for the revelation of God's name, of his transcendent presence in the world, and where in a world of empirical phenomena of which he is himself a part, Jesus stands for the paradoxical incarnation of God's word, a word which as the eschaton is audible only in faith which is iconoclastic because its only "reality" is eschatological.

## 3

The word is an icon. But its function is always an iconoclastic function (Matt. 26/61; Mark 14/58; John 2/19). This amounts to saying that, like dogmatism or literalism, meaninglessness is ultimately no option at all, if only because in the last analysis iconoclasm is a protest against their objectifying tendency to construe authentic life in continuity with empirical life. Without going back to the classical period, one may say that in the history of Western culture this protest once was identified with the function of theology. Theology desacralized the world and spiritualized it: the cost was the secularization of Christianity. As a result, theology has now ceased to be the voice of this protest; the iconoclastic function of the word has been assumed, if not usurped, by secularistic ideologies weaned on the word and, in particular, by literature, the orphan of the orphans of the word.

The word iconoclasm is used here in what may be considered to be its biblical sense, which greatly differs from its common usage.[20] Basically, the common meaning of iconoclasm refers either to the anti-artistic drive of every kind of religious or ideological puritanism, or to the Promethean or blasphemous revolts against theism, against God as the reality which calls into being the reality of man. Promethean iconoclasm construes man in terms of autonomy by attempting, in vain, to reject all heteronomy. Biblical iconoclasm overcomes this antinomy and dissolves in fact all this-worldly antinomies. Thus the myth of the creation, by pointing to the radical difference between the creator and the creature, makes human freedom not only a rhetorical but an actual possibility. To say that man is not God does not steal freedom away from man but asserts and endows it with the dignity that behooves its frailty. Therefore biblical iconoclasm is directed, not against God, but against idolatry in all its forms from superstition to legalism or dogmatism and literalism—against anything that preaches the deification of man, the divinization of culture or history or reason and religion as well as against anything that sacralizes symbolic events or institutions. Because biblical iconoclasm thus centers on the idea that theonomy alone can authenticate the verbal nature of reality, it finds its classic expression in the figure of Abraham, the father of faith, the knight of faith.

Indeed, the Old Testament's understanding of faith as Abrahamic iconoclasm corresponds to the New Testament's understanding of faith as eschatological existence. It is this kind of iconoclasm which not only is at work in Jesus' words about the Sabbath or the Temple but is also in point of fact the cause of the final accusation brought against him. It lies at the heart of the controversy at Antioch. And, later on, whereas in the name of this same principle medieval Christendom constitutes a protest both against the sacredness of nature and against religious and intellectual isolationism, the Reformation (through its motto *ecclesia reformata semper reformanda*) constitutes for its part a protest against the idolatrous claim of ecclesiastic sacredness in terms of which the world was ultimately rejected except insofar as it was subordinated to a supernatural world. But throughout, one and the same dilemma confronts this iconoclastic faith; how to "spiritualize" the world without secularizing Christianity. The secularization of the Christian tradition reaches its nadir in the death of God, a phenomenon which, regardless of how desperately one wishes to blame Promethean, or blasphemous metaphysical rebellion, reveals to what extent Christianity, by fostering and finally surrendering to secularism, had forfeited its iconoclastic vocation in the modern period.

It is not surprising therefore that the birth of the post-Christian era coincides with the transfer of the iconoclastic tradition—though perhaps mutilated—from theology to literature, even to Promethean literature. In the wake of this transfer, the traditional conflict between theism and atheism, no longer supported by a transcendentalist framework, has evaporated. The idolatry of religion itself being laid bare, the way is open to the possibility of understanding in a fresh manner the biblical notion that transcendent as God's reality may be, it must be attested in the world and its empirical phenomena through the structures of human existence, of man's works and his word:

> But it seems that something has happened that
> has never happened before: though we know
> not just when, or why, or how, or where.
> Men have left GOD not for other gods, they say,
> but for no god; and this has never happened
> before
> That men both deny gods and worship gods,
> professing first Reason,
> And then Money, and Power, and what they call
> Life, or Race, or Dialectic.[21]

> . . . the Church is no longer regarded, not even
> opposed, and men have forgotten
> All gods except Usury, Lust and Power.[22]

> O Father . . . . . . . .
> The heathen are come into thine inheritance.[23]

Accordingly, the death of God not only liberates Christianity from ethnolatry as well as faith from the idolatry of religion; it also means that iconoclastic faith has no proper sphere of action other than *secularity*. As a cultural phenomenon, the death of God thus points to the fact that eschatological existence is not one aspect of the human reality but pervades it through and through, even to the point of seemingly becoming completely secular if that should be the only means of preserving the iconoclastic function of the word as an icon.

That is to say, by Westernizing God, by objectifying the

Church and faith into empirical data of this world, Christianity has turned the God of Abraham, of Jacob, of Isaac, the God of Jesus Christ into an unknown God that man, even modern man, would serve if only he could know that this God is the Wholly Other:

> I would know thee, thou Unknown One,
> Who dost lay hold of my soul in its depths,
> Moving through my life like a storm,
> Incomprehensible, and yet kin to me!
> I would know thee, and even serve thee![24]

## 4

Though the preceding comments no doubt need to be further clarified, they may suffice to permit us to deny that there is any valid dichotomy between the sphere of religion and the sphere of literature. That is to say, I am no more interested in subsuming literature under religion than I am in subsuming religion under literature—or, like Matthew Arnold and Santayana, under poetry. Nor am I concerned with literature as a moralistic or apologetic tool—as though it were to be viewed as a vast fresco of the sinfulness of man without God—or as art for art's sake, a futile and inconsistent conception except insofar as such a view is espoused to protest against the opposite conception of literature as apologetics or as propaganda. On the other hand, when Trotsky, for example, proclaims that the literature of the future will be atheistic, he forgets what he otherwise seems to know, namely that, whether atheistic or theistic, if literature should cease to incarnate the two-fold iconoclastic function of the word—as consent or as dissent—it will have altogether ceased to be.

One can agree with T. S. Eliot's statement that all religious literature constitutes "a pious insincerity";[25] and infer that all sincere literature is therefore religious.

Furthermore, the question whether the creative act of the novelist or of the poet is in some sense an echo of the divine act of creation or the denial of the divine creation—an attempt to remake the world—is not our problem in the present context. In other words, we are not concerned here with the question whether man's creative act is a reproduction or a representation, or seeks to be a correction, of the divine creation.

In the book of Genesis when God creates the animals and Adam names them, God binds himself to man's word and limits his creative word. His Word assumes the word of man, not because there is no difference between them, but precisely because there is no divine Word apart from man's sacramental word: " . . . whatever the man called every living creature, that was its name. The man gave names to all the cattle, and to the birds of the air, and to every beast of the field." (Gen. 2/19–20.) But simply naming the animals (i.e., art for art's sake), though it were enough to show one's assent to the reality of the world, would still be meaningless: this I take to be the meaning of that strange appendix to Adam's naming of all living creatures: "but for the man there was not found a helper fit for him" (Gen. 2/20), as if the finding of a helper were the purpose of it all!

Indeed, by being given dominion over the creation, Adam in no way duplicates God but realizes that this dominion does not prevent him from being simultaneously dependent upon the creation, as well as utterly dependent upon God. Adam's creativity only reveals his humanity. And his word does not bring anything about, but merely confirms the fact that the animals are there, and does so, moreover, in a rather gratuitous, arbitrary manner.

Essentially, the word of man is even nonsensical. It does not add form to matter in any attempt whatever to grasp the reality of the cosmos, as the Greeks would have it. Even while corroborating the creative Word of God, human speech can never do so without running the risk of culminating in a tower of Babel. Speech will never enable man to "imitate," i.e., imagine and represent, or confess God without being first overcome by Pentecost. Otherwise, God and man would be either confused or arbitrarily separated as if the difference between them were merely quantitative.

Indeed, an analogy of their qualitative difference is to be found in the fact that words can only make sense in relation to another person, to others. They are reminders of one's humanity, as Adam is reminded of his in the incongruous awareness that there was no helper fit for him. Let us be more specific.

Through language man both overcomes the indifference if not the hostility of the world as natural occurrence, and establishes its verbal nature, even while embodying his dependence on it—a dependence, however, that cannot, because it equally reveals Adam's need for a helper, be quantitatively measured or serve as the basis for any kind of empirical revelation of the human reality. Consequently, it is not man who is understood in terms of the world but, rather, the world is understood in terms of man. And, inasmuch as the world, that is, the deed of God's Word, thus becomes the sphere of man's word, language also testifies to the "empirical" givenness of God, although never in such a way as to reduce God to a single characteristic of reality or to the totality of its characteristics. Finally, that the nature of reality is verbal implies the impossibility, even empirically, of eliminating God's reality as well as of reducing the human reality to an empirical phenomenon. In itself, the world is meaningless. Nor can this statement be valid unless it also implies that God's reality is both *given* with, and *other* than, the reality of the world as well as the act of existence. Put differently, the reality of the world does not yield any meaning, any idea of the Supreme Good or Beauty, since the creation itself, being "never conceived after the analogy of a work (ἔργον) or a product of craftmanship (τέχνη)"[26] is what distinguishes without separating the reality of God from that of man. On the basis of this kind of otherness alone can man speak, in contrast to God, who speaks the word and it is done.

## 5

Indeed, "with God word and deed are one: his speaking is the way of his acting."[27] God speaks and the thing happens (Ps. 33/9). " . . . So shall my word be that goes forth from my mouth; it shall not return to me empty, but it shall accomplish that which I purpose, and prosper in the thing for which I sent it" (Isa. 55/11). "All things were made through (the word), and without him was not anything made that was made" (John 1/3). "By faith we understand that the world was created by the word of God, so that what is seen was made out of things which do not appear" (Heb. 11/3). By contrast, the word of man "cannot make one hair black or white" (Matt. 5/36); for this reason, Jesus adds: "Let what you say be simply 'Yes' or 'No'; anything more than this comes from evil" (Matt. 5/37; cf. James 5/12). Hence the language of man at the least is "an ambiguous blend of Yes and No" (II Cor. 1/18), like an icon, like a symbol which both points to and is not that which is symbolized.

But a symbol which does not hark back to, or assert, empirical reality is a convention. Likewise, when language becomes a mere convention of signs and sounds, it robs the human reality of its verbal nature, of its charismatic power to be with others and never to be without God. Language, therefore, is symbolic and can communicate only where there is communion. Communication, communion, being-with-others—being is ultimately the text of which language is the expression, the translation, the ambiguous Yes and No. Instead, we have today become "accustomed to think of words chiefly as bearers of a definite sense, of a content of ideas." Consequently,

> we too easily overlook the fact that the real power and significance of words lie in their effecting something, aiming at something, even when it is just a matter of "information," and quite certainly in the mode in

> which more than information is communicated, when one communicates himself to another, and so by means of words there takes place a "having together with the other." Meeting in the deepest sense is not something that takes place apart and separated from words, but it happens in the event of speech.[28]

But language is also an "abstraction in that it does not manifest reality," though it may signify it, "in and through truth,"[29] in and through being. Language is an abstraction in the sense that it produces nothing, except its meaning and even then there is something "gratuitous" about it, as Ricoeur remarks.[30] "It can state, question, invoke, and at the same time say nothing, or lie and deceive, or babble. Hamlet dies saying: Words! Words! Words!"[31] Is it any wonder, then, that a contemporary writer should identify literature as an *activité de mort* inasmuch as literature "succeeds only because it results in books, but fails because it can do nothing for or against the real"?[32] A strange way, is it not, of ultimately denying literature in the very name of literature?

Because the real is verbal, both realism and formalism (like autonomy and heteronomy) are bound to flounder, inasmuch as they both tame, in one way or another, the iconoclastic function of the word. As Father Lynch says:

> We are all driven by a need for maximum beauty and insight, and at the same time we wish for a habitation in the inescapable minima of human life. Yet we cannot tolerate a permanent dissociation between the two. We wish on the one hand to grasp "meaning" to the full, so that there is no pain of questioning left; on the other hand we have an equal longing for pure, unalloyed, concrete objects, and for not having to go beyond them to get a meaning, joy or illumination. This double longing exists in all of us. We want the unlimited and the dream, and we also want the earth.[33]

We want the icon, but not its iconoclastic function. We want the deed that reveals our word—our being, even as the world reveals the majesty and the glory of God's word,[34] unconscious as we are of the fact that such a deed is precisely the Word of God. And so we want to become like God or, what amounts to the same thing, we crave for a principle of explanation which would not be affected by the relativities of empirical data, oblivious as we are to the fact that the reality of God is indeed an "empirical phenomenon" of the world, provided that the reality of the world, however, as a verbal phenomenon is itself predicated on its being the deed of God's word. As Paul says: men "in their wickedness are stifling the truth" though "all that may be known of God . . . lies before their eyes" and though "God himself has disclosed it to them" (Rom. 1/18–20).

## 6

Expressive of the verbal nature of reality, the word should have been sufficient to establish man in his own authenticity but is instead the channel through which this authenticity leaks. Indeed, the word should not even need the light of any revealed word to authenticate man's deed, just as conversely no special revelation is needed for the word of man to pulverize man's deed. That is to say, God as the Word is not a necessary part of human speech, is not essential to it; or else the reality of God could not be apprehended as an empirical phenomenon. Nor could the Word become flesh. And it becomes flesh neither by adding to nor subtracting from man's word some kind of dimension whereby this word will recover the iconoclastic vocation of its authenticating power: "There is no other light shining in Jesus than has always already shined in the creation."[35] Accordingly, to confess that "*Christ* is revelation and that revelation is the *word*"[36] also implies that God's Word lies in man's word and, on the other hand, that revelation is "an *occurrence*, and not a communication of supernatural knowledge";[37] that is to say, "revelation does not mediate a worldview,"[38] an objective quantification of the word, like culture in general and literature in particular and like moral achievement in the contemplation of which "we really only discover ourselves, or at best, an image of what we ought to be and can be."[39]

Thus, what prevents me from becoming an object among other objects, from identifying authentic, i.e., eschatological, existence with a series of empirical data, is the word; or rather, it *should be* the word. For the word can prevent me from that only when it is itself freed by the Word of God, only because the Word of God belongs to the word of man: man's word is the flesh of God's Word. As human speech, literature can hence be said genuinely to aim at transfiguring the world and depicting man's situation "before God." Not that in such a situation man is in need of God (God is not a want, a lack). With or without God man is before God; and the word, regardless of how meaningless it has become, still and always is what questions man's deeds, and taxes the magnificence of his works; and denudes them, and their nakedness shows that they are mere words.

As Paul puts it, "The kingdom of God does not consist in talk (ἐν λόγῳ) but in power" (I Cor. 4/20), yet this power is the power of the word, the power of the kingdom as the word that addresses us through our words (cf. Matt. 13/19). "I tell you, on the day of judgement men will render account for every careless word they utter; for by your words you will be justified, and by your words you will be condemned" (Matt. 12/36–37), inasmuch as "you have been born anew . . . through the living and enduring word of God" (I Pet. 1/23). As Ebeling writes: "Even the most splendid things in man, including his religiousness, without the Holy Spirit are simply 'flesh.' But on the other hand, even the most significant and unpretentious things in human life are destined to be the instrument of the Spirit. For the gift of the Spirit is no more than the pledge of what the Spirit as Sanctifier is able to effect in man, to the point of the resurrection from the dead."[40]

## 7

What then is the word? Something that means something but does not accomplish anything. And this remains true even when it is made to convey propaganda, whether religious or political. The time always comes when the vanity of the word lays bare all our pretensions, our idolatrous proclivity as well as our natural inclination toward self-apotheosis, or toward the apotheosis of our cultural achievements and our religious securities, or toward ethnolatry or idolatry. Though the word, more exactly through the vanity of the word, the world is recognized as world and the flesh as flesh, and life is affirmed as a gift, as a mandate. Our systems of thought, theological, philosophical, aesthetic, or otherwise, our political dreams and our social programs suddenly appear as the unwarranted amplification of an overconfidence in the power of the word, in the process of which its inherent weakness, its vanity is overlooked. Indeed, the history of the word, of literature—religious and otherwise—is the history of man's adaptation to the world, of his adoption of the world, and also of his refusal to surrender to exigencies of objectification with which his adoption of the world necessarily confronts him. Through the word, culture thus expresses man's legitimate refusal of adaptation, and becomes also, as Ricoeur points out, that which disadapts man and holds him ready and open for the future, for the other.[41] This is what we call the iconoclastic function of the word: it enables man to conceive his being as a project but prevents him ultimately from identifying it with the realization of this project, from being saved by his works as if "eternal life" were "a phenomenon of this life," though "in a certain sense it is already present" in this life.[42] The word provides man with a home and a city, and tells him at the same time that here is no abiding city. It is by faith that Abraham "sojourned in the land of promise, as in a foreign land" (Heb. 11/9). As Auden puts it, in a somewhat laconic fashion:

> Life is fleeting and full of sorrow and no words can prevent the brave and beautiful from dying or annihilate a grief. What poetry can do is transform the real world into an imaginary one which is god-like in its permanence and beauty, providing a picture of life which is worthy of imitations as far as it is possible. It is not possible, of course, but without the attempt the real world would get even worse.[43]

## 8

The word is what brings into evidence the reality of the world, and does so by expressing the verbal nature of this reality.[44] I call verbal, for example, the "baptismal" property of water in contrast to the conceptual cleansing property of $H_2O$. And in this connection, it is not for nothing that, in the sacramental practice of the Church, baptism is considered as being properly administered and therefore as valid only if the baptismal formula is pronounced at the same time as water is being poured. It is because reality has a verbal dimension that its elements can become the symbolic instruments by which meaning is transferred from one object to another, from one being to another—by which language is not merely *flatus vocis.*

The world is what takes place in and through the word. Without the word, the world is powerless. This same powerlessness is what Paul speaks of in his epistle to the Romans when he refers to the groaning of the creation. That Paul's phrase should seem, from our technological post-Christian vantage point, to be just a metaphor simply points, if not to the dire poverty of our own desiccated capacity for the word, at least to the groaning of our own language, to modern man's groping, however unconscious, for the metaphoric instrumentality of the word, without which the "being of men" cannot be "founded in language."[45]

A metaphor, Aristotle says in his *Poetics*, consists in transferring the name of one object to another.[46] What interests me in this definition is that it makes calling a spade a spade itself a metaphor as it does also of the commandment which forbids the transfer of God's name to any other reality than God: "Thou shalt not make graven images," or "Thou shalt not take my name in vain." Even more interesting, however, is the fact that the metaphoric function of language points to the primordial nature of reality as resilient both to autonomy and heteronomy, to subjectivism and objectivism, or to the false immanentism of literalism, materialism, and positivism. And in this light, incidentally, it may easily be seen how religious otherworldliness defies the fact of the world's sacramental coinherence just as this-worldliness defies the fact of the world's incoherence.[47]

The metaphoric power of the word, the transference of the name of one object to another does not mean that the properties of the one are transferred to the other; nor does it mean that the new world which is then brought about becomes the property of my word, any more than the Word of God—that supreme metaphor of the meaningfulness of human speech—becomes the property of the word of man: "My thoughts are not your thoughts, neither are your ways my ways, says the Lord" (Isa. 55/8). Otherwise, the metaphor clots into a cliché or a dogma as the case is when the Word of God becomes identified with a certain human form of speech, and faith with certain standards of belief or practices, even while the world becomes the scene of man's estrangement. As Heidegger puts it: "The presence of the gods and the appearance of the world are not merely a consequence of the actualization of language, they are contemporaneous with it."[48] Or, as the Decalogue itself states: "Thou shalt have no other Gods before me"; that is to say, there is no other God than the wholly other God whose reality can be attested by no graven images, no frozen or absolute metaphors, for the simple reason, indeed, that his reality is given with "the actualization of language," with the fact of existence, even the empirical irreducibility of the human phenomenon. Indeed what is a graven image but the symbolic reduction of the metaphoric power of the word, the denial of the iconoclastic instrumentality of human existence as word?

## 9

The word is an icon—not a graven image, and not a static or logical symbol. And the word is an icon only when it is iconoclastic.[49] It is no wonder, therefore, that like faith poetry is most iconoclastic when it most tends toward the pure metaphor, the silent word; i.e., when our words speak in spite of their speechlessness, because then they are assumed by the Word:

> The winds are strong! flesh is brief! . . .
>
> . . . . . . . . . . . . . . .
>
> O Poet, O bilingual one, amidst all things two-pronged, and you, yourself, litigation amid all things litigious—man unassailed by the god! man speaking in the equivocal! . . . ah! like a man entangled in a mêlée of wings and brambles, among nuptials of harrier-eagles!
>
> And you, Sun from below, ferocity of the Being with no eyelids, hold your puma's eye in all this conglomerate of precious stones! . . . Hazardous is the enterprise on which I have led the course of this song . . . And still there is cause for suspicion. But the Wind, ah! the Wind! its power is without design and of itself enamoured.
>
> We pass on, and our shadows . . . Great works, page by page, great works are silently composed in the breeding-places of the future, in the whiteness of blind broodings. From there we take our new writings, from the layered pages of great schists . . .
>
> . . . . . . . . . . . . . . .
>
> And the red hands are prophesying on the beggar's bed of stone knives. And on the sigillated soil, the texts

> are revealed. And that is quite true, I call truth to witness. And you may say to me: Where did you see that? . . . More than one mask is forming on the brows of the tall limestones, dazzled with presence.[50]

Language, Heidegger writes, always endangers "what is most characteristic of it, the genuine saying," simply because "the word as word never gives any direct guarantee as to whether it is an essential word or a counterfeit," and because "an essential word often looks in its simplicity like an unessential one."[51] What makes a word essential is neither its adequacy to what it names nor the adequacy of the thing named to the intellect. A word becomes essential only when it can inhabit, or receive, another word, only when it calls out the neighborhood of another word, of words. It is in this sense that we can understand Mallarmé's dictum that a poem is made with words, not with ideas. A poem emerges from the co-inhabitation of words. And that is why in a good poem no word is unessential, and yet the poem happens in spite of the words. By contrast, ideas and concepts, and to some extent symbols, mainly serve to carry information or to perpetuate and thus "homogenize" and by the same token violate the transfiguration of reality mediated by the poem, by the word. Ideas, concepts, and perhaps symbols too, are to the word as the booths that Peter wanted to build on the Mount of Transfiguration are to the words "This is my beloved son," which leave the disciples confronted with no one else but Jesus, our unessential words assumed by the Word (Mark 9/2 ff.; Matt. 17/1 ff).

## 10

Let us go back to Aristotle. Even his definition, colliding as it does with the commandment prohibiting graven images, can be used to throw light on the fact that if a metaphor consists in the assumption of our words by the metaphor we call the Word of God, God himself becomes a metaphor, even though the supreme metaphor and, then, either God or the metaphor is dead. Language, indeed, is often nothing but a dead metaphor. This happens when the word ceases to be iconoclastic, when the word no longer is an icon, or when it is no longer "bilingual" as Saint-John Perse says of the poet, and becomes a graven image.

A graven image is a word identifying itself *with* the reality it names: it identifies the Word of God with the appearances of God's works. Such an identification, however, is precisely what denies the claim that with God word and deed are one, for they are one only in the sense that the deed is what the Word says, not the Word itself. Thus, to say that man is created in the image of God makes no sense without its corollary, the imagelessness of God. Indeed, the general revelation of God in and through his creation never meant that God's reality was a piece of the reality of the world.[52] For, as the Wisdom of Solomon puts it, men are "unable from the good things that are seen to know him who exists," nor do they "recognize the craftsman while paying heed to his works," but they suppose that "either fire or wind or swift air, or the circle of the stars, or turbulent water, or the luminaries of heaven [are] the gods that rule the world." Indeed, though "from the greatness and beauty of created things comes a corresponding perception of their Creator," men "live among his works" and "trust what they see" (Wisd. of Sol. 13/1–9). Owen Barfield has expressed the point we are making by saying that "when the 'things' of the physical world have become idols, then indeed the literal interpretation excludes the symbolic, and *vice versa*."[53] In other terms, by virtue of its proper metaphoric function, the word precludes both literalism and "symbolism"; it precludes semantic or aesthetic and mystical positivism, revelational or gnostic positivism; or, in more theological categories, the word averts both sacramentalism and spiritualism.[54] Indeed, because the sacramental power of the world is coextensive with its verbal nature, this power is only charismatic: it lies in its readiness for the word as well as in its accessibility to the word. In and of itself the world has no meaning other than that by which man is confirmed in his natural propensity to idolatry, to self-contradiction, to that mode of being which would constitute man as his own contradiction, as a "useless passion" or *flatus vocis,* were it not for the fact that the word is an icon (regardless of how devalued an icon it is) or that man himself, as Saint Paul says, is "the image (ἐίκων) and the glory of God" (I Cor. 11/7).

*God is a word,* the word that our words do not speak unless they are shocked both out of their literal and out of their symbolic meaning.

Through the metaphor the word of man shows that this is possible. And this cannot be possible unless its reality is given with its possibility, unless the Word of God is given with the occurrence of that reality. Today our words are either symbolic or literal: either way their form is their content—a definition which stands in flagrant contradiction with my definition of the word as an icon. Such aesthetic reductionism is merely another instance of the general surrender to immanentism which is characteristic of our time, and results either from the divorce between the literal and the symbolic or from their conflation, their confusion. Religious symbolism makes no sense today precisely because it cannot be communicated except with words and images that have lost their metaphoric power, or that have been severed from the metaphoric power of the word of man. A faith which has been drained of its iconoclastic vocation can only wallow in words and images that cheat man into idolatry instead of confirming him as an iconoclast.

## 11

To sum up, we have spoken indiscriminately of religion and literature as if they were one and the same thing, and we have done this from the point of view of a theological distinction between the Word of God and the word of man. However, we have not simply relied on the contention that theology has secular implications, or that it is itself a secular mode of speech, and that correspondingly secular literature always has a theological dimension. Nor have we been merely claiming that there is no antinomy between the secular and the religious, the sacred and the profane.

From the theological distinction between the Word of God and the word of man one can only draw the following conclusion, namely: the concept itself of a sacred Scripture could not hold unless there were no such thing as a sacred language, a sacred word: just this we may take to be the meaning of the biblical canon. The Word of God does not communicate a worldview, a body of supernatural knowledge, but addresses me in my own words—and of course it is not possible even to make such a statement without the mediation of some "sacred" revelation, whether the latter is a body of scripture or tradition. The Bible itself is not the Word of God; it contains that Word. It does not create but witnesses to the Word of God; it preaches the Word of God in spite of itself, not because it is sacred. In and of itself it cannot make this happen.

Now then, what is the Word of God, since it does not "designate a complex of statements that can be found and understood with respect to their 'content'?"[55]

To raise this kind of question means to think of God's reality in terms of some objectifying conceptuality according to which this reality would be something up there, or out there, or within me, i.e., a natural phenomenon of this world. The Word of God is what happens when God speaks and the thing happens, when the creation points to the infinite qualitative difference between itself and the creator, when "the word, the word of God, which we ourselves shall never speak, has put on our weakness and unprofitableness so that *our* word *in* its very weakness and unprofitableness has become capable at least of becoming the mortal frame, the earthen vessel, of the word of God."[56] When this happens, the Word of God is not what the word of man is lacking, any more than the reality of God is the missing link of the human reality, but what affirms man; that is, the possibility of saying what the Word of God is, of hearing the Word of God, is itself the Word of God, and this is what is meant by confessing Christ as the Word of God incarnate.

Consequently, we are not concerned with any attempt to differentiate between theology and literature, between theological literature and secular literature, by claiming, for example, that theological literature takes the word as its subject whereas secular literature takes it as its object. This would amount to introducing a false, a mystical or supernatural dichotomy between the Word of God and the word of man, resting on merely an epistemological understanding of their differences and resulting therefore in the Word of God becoming a conceptuality differing from human conceptualities only quantitatively. To speak thus of the Word of God is precisely sin. For the word of man is just where God's word becomes flesh.

# Calvin: Theology and The Death of God

Let the sea roar, and all that fills it;
the world and those who dwell in it!
Let the floods clap their hands;
let the hills sing for joy together
before the Lord, for he comes
to rule the earth.
He will judge the world with righteousness,
and the peoples with equity.

(Ps. 98/7–9)

# V

## Calvin: Theology and The Death of God

THE QUESTION WHETHER OR NOT THEOLOGY IS AN AUTONOMOUS, ecclesiastical science is a false question. Theology is truly ecclesiastical only to the extent that it is open to and assumes the world and its wisdom, only to the extent that it asserts the worldliness of that world of which, for want of the Church, God is always the contemporary. In Christ eternity itself, so to speak, becomes dated, the word becomes flesh. Even the Bible, unless it be idolatrously equated with the Word of God, does not witness to, or proclaim this Word otherwise than through human words as well as in spite of them. Clearly, the Bible itself points as much to the theologian's intellectual dependence on the wisdom of the world as to his independence from it. The more theology is biblical, the more it will take seriously the twin exigency of homogeneity and heterogeneity in relation to any given situation in which it must operate. Theology is no sacred science: it used to be the channel through which the world understood itself as church and through which the Church asserted the reality of the world. Rather, theology is that critical and self-critical task of faith in terms of which the world understands itself as church and the Church manifests the reality of the world. What prevents theology from dissolving itself into an immanentist ideology is precisely what the tradition called, in the strict sense, theo–logy.

To claim that theology is primarily an ecclesiastical discipline implies that the Church is merely one institution among others and has therefore ceased to be "in" the world; it has become a part of the world or, rather, a vestige of an outdated worldview. Lest God be an atavism and the Word of God an archeological language, the theologian must speak the dialect of his contemporaries: the greatness of theology is its heel of Achilles. In discharging its obligation to bespeak and celebrate God's contemporaneity with man, it becomes vulnerable.

Today, theology is not merely vulnerable, it is questionable. The dawn of a post-Christian age seems to make theology implausible, and renders all allegiance to our theological tradition uncomfortable and somewhat contrived if not outright fraudulent.

Indeed, the possibility itself of theology is in question. Can one do theology at all? And if so what kind of theological inquiry can still be valid today? Fully aware of the obsolescence inherent in every theological discourse, let us consider the two-fold question—whether theology is an intellectual option at all and what is its relevance to a post-Christian cultural situation—in the light of Calvin's theology. For this purpose, let us first try to assess the Reformer's theology from the standpoint of our post-Christian era, then attempt to interpret what Calvin had to say to *his* contemporaries. In this light, we can finally seek to define the possibility of theological existence against the background of the present cultural consciousness of the death of God.

## 1

Most important to a proper understanding of our theme is the necessity to take into account the post-Christian nature of our contemporary situation in order not only to point out what implications this has for faith but also to show what theological method is today possible inasmuch we have no choice but to abide by the rule of methodological atheism.

We are not pleading here for a new theological reformation, more or less patterned after that of the sixteenth century. At that time, only Christendom was moribund—not the faith; or else there would have been no re*form*ation. After all, in spite of some major differences, the Reformation stood in basic agreement with the tradition of the medieval Church as well as with that of the early Church and of the New Testament. The Reformers did not have to contend with the *cultural* relevance of the Christian faith to their contemporaries, but rather with the question of what language would adequately mediate the contemporaneity of faith with their historical situation.

What makes our historical situation different from that of the Reformers is that it is post-Christian, by which we mean that our alienation from the Christian tradition is not only religious, but also cultural. That is why a new reformation alone would not suffice to render theology relevant to our situation, if this reformation is not itself predicated on the antecedent necessity of a cultural revolution. In other words, *our dilemma is not so much spiritual or ecclesiastical as it is secular.* There is no congruence between the spiritual order as it is still represented by our traditional institutions and conceptualities and the secular order in which we live and which has emancipated itself both from the ecclesiastical culture of the Middle Ages and the theological culture of the Reformation. Our question, accordingly, no longer is, as with the Reformers, how we must interpret this or that ancient doctrine. That would imply a fundamental agreement between the preconception of one intellectual climate and that of another. But to say that our age is post-Christian means to acknowledge the emergence of a self-understanding based on such a radically different type of preconception that if it is taken into consideration, as it must be, then one must concede that the preconception on which the

Christian worldview rests has been neutralized, and is now irretrievable.

This alone would make it necessary for theology first and foremost to outgrow its Christian biblical worldview. Actually, as Bultmann contends, biblical thought itself compels the theologian to do so, insofar as such an adjustment is not merely a concession to the world but is dictated by the exigencies of faith, fundamental to which is the notion that, whatever the difference of pre-understanding and existential conceptualities, the question of man *mutatis mutandis* remains essentially the same throughout the ages. What faith has to contend with, then, is not the question itself of the human phenomenon in its empirical givenness but the ideology that inevitably deflects it one way or the other. Thus, during the Christian era faith had to contend with transcendentalism and its degeneration into otherworldliness—a type of otherworldliness which, for all its piety, bespeaks the loss of God's transcendent presence in the world. Today, faith has to contend with secularism and its denial not of the transcendence but of the immanence of God.

Governing our worldview and our self-understanding thus is what, by way of contrast, may be called radical immanentism. This kind of immanentism, which has nothing to do with classical metaphysical immanentism, leaves God altogether out of the picture and must be understood in the sense of what is implied, for example, by the notion of immanent justice rather than by any of the various notions of God's immanence. Whether God is or is not, radical immanentism considers him at best irrelevant, and seeks accordingly to define existence and the world without the help of a transcendental reference. The least that can be said is that radical immanentism is worlds apart from the world of the Bible and seeks to justify modern man's divorce from traditional theology as well as his cultural inaptitude for the Christian faith.

How could we possibly agree, for example, with Calvin's

definition according to which "the theologian's task is not to divert the ears with chatter, but to strengthen consciences by teaching things true, sure and profitable,"[1] in other words, to establish and spell out a specific sum of knowledge? Or, when he writes that "the knowledge of faith consists more in certainty than in apprehension"[2]—even if by that he means that faith is "a firm and certain knowledge of God's benevolence toward us, founded upon the truth of the freely given promise in Christ, both revealed to our minds and sealed upon our hearts through the Holy Spirit"[3]—is not Calvin actually intellectualizing faith, and is he not historicizing eschatology? And is that why theology is for him a practical science?

Nor is he concerned with any kind of tension between reason and revelation, especially when he contends that the general knowledge of God can only scuttle itself and make way for the knowledge of revelation—must scuttle itself, moreover, because Adam did not "persist in his state of integrity."[4] All we get by way of an explanation is the statement that the knowledge of God "is that by which we not only conceive that there is a God but also grasp what befits us and is proper to his glory, in fine, what is to our advantage to know of him. Indeed, we shall not say that properly speaking, God is known where there is no religion or piety."[5] In an age which claims to be non-religious are we finally to witness the truth of Wendel's prediction made a few decades ago when he declared that "Calvin's *Institutes* will be read in the twentieth century even less than in the nineteenth?"[6] Is not the purpose of the *Institutes* to impart a theology of existence and of history, the documents for which are promulgated by the creation itself, are attested by that "awareness of divinity" which is innate in every man, and are to be interpreted in the light of Scripture? Against the background of today's secularism, it is hard to see how, in spite of some major differences, Calvin's Christian philosophy could have differed in its assumptions and presuppositions from that general religiosity of the Christian tradition which "colonized" the world and enregimented natural man into the brigades of heaven.

For example, the doctrine of predestination, which to be sure makes no sense apart from Jesus Christ, is nevertheless the justification for Calvin's theory of civil government—and its subsequent secularization. It is not altogether by accident that the *Institutes* terminates with considerations on political theory. In fact, with Calvin, the *civitas terrena* has already become such a replica of the *civitas Dei* that subsequently this kind of realized eschatology will give way to historical immanentist utopianism, and thereby prove both itself and its subject matter generally irrelevant to the concrete situation of man.

Calvin's theology seems, indeed, to be a theology that seeks to "prove" itself, as Barth would say, and correspondingly either proves or invalidates itself—or both. Unless, of course, what Calvin said to his contemporaries has been misunderstood.

The fact is that the Calvin we still read and seem to, or wish to, consider pertinent is not related to the fundamental nature of our present crisis, which is essentially cultural. And yet Calvin himself was the founder of a new civilization. We look to him as the fountainhead of a spiritual and even an economic byproduct, but we are totally blind to the fact that for him faith meant secularity (not secularism), i.e., involvement in the world. The world was for him a place of pilgrimage. For us, it is the Church which has become a place of nostalgic pilgrimage.

Let us not forget that, though Calvin tends to objectivize faith and historicize eschatology, what prevents him from altogether surrendering eschatology to history is his claim that if faith as eschatological existence must not be identified *with* empirical existence, it must nevertheless be identified *through* empirical existence. Even *qua* knowledge, faith is for him "a different thing from knowledge."[7] Consistently, his emphasis falls on the assertion that, whether man is a sinner or, *a fortiori*, whether he is not, salvation depends on

God: "We must be assured that God will continue his goodness toward us. And we must not doubt when he has begun to manifest himself as savior that he will do so till the end. When we thus grasp him we must hence go on trusting that we can call upon him throughout our life. For otherwise we should be saved only for a day, and that might as well be as if God had never revealed himself to us. Our hope must accordingly extend to the future" so that we may enjoy God's heritage.[8]

With this in mind let us briefly sketch what Calvin says to his contemporaries and then make a few comments about his method.

## 2

Without even so much as the briefest introduction, Calvin states that self-knowledge precedes all knowledge except itself. He declares in the very first paragraph of the *Institutes:* "True and substantial wisdom principally consists of two parts, the knowledge of God and the knowledge of ourselves. But, while these two branches of knowledge are so intimately connected, which of them precedes and produces the other is not easy to discover."[9] "Accordingly," Calvin adds, "the knowledge of ourselves not only arouses us to seek God (*à cognoistre Dieu*), but also, as it were, leads us by the hand to find him."[10] It is God alone who can, as Zwingli said, reveal man to himself. In other words, only where it is a question of God is man himself in question; and where it is a question of man, the only question is that of God.

What kind of God? Not, as we shall see again later on, the God of philosophers and savants; but the God of Abraham, of Isaac, of Jacob, the God who in Jesus Christ assumes the form of man—and lets me assume the form of a man, of the particular man that I am. Knowledge, either of God or of ourselves, has thus nothing to do either with rational and "frivolous speculations" about the existence or the nature of God or with the nature of man.[11] For Calvin the doctrine of God does not revolve around the question, *Quid sit Deus?* but *Qualis sit Deus?*[12] The difference is important and not merely a matter of terminology. It explains why Calvin's understanding of the "nature" of man is so diverse and so fluctuating that, it might be said, he does not even have one. Indeed, those who have one as their premise are the sociologists, the psychologists, the philosophers, the economists, in a word, those who have no need for theology and who *ipso facto* precisely justify the task of the theologian—provided of course that the theologian wants to be a theologian and not a sociologist, or a psychologist, a philosopher, or an economist, in a word, one of those for whom self-knowledge would be self-sufficient and self-authenticating. For this reason, Calvin holds that in order to know himself man must know himself as one known by God.

To understand oneself means to stand under God. And who can stand before God, but the man who is at once sinful and justified? Justification by faith thus means that man need no longer be sinless in order to stand before God. Or to permit an extrapolation that may clarify this point: the human nature need not be "transubstantiated" in order to stand revealed to itself. That is to say, if self-knowledge is not autonomous, it is not heteronomous either. The man who accepts himself is not accepting just himself: where it is a question of man, indeed, it is also a question of God. Justification by faith thus means that the question of God does not violate the question of man, but makes it in fact possible, even where no possibility is in view: God deals with man as if man deserved to be saved; and man is not saved by what he does but by what God does.

How do we know that the question of man, that assuming one's contingency or taking the form of man, is possible? We know it in Jesus Christ: by which is meant no invitation to a flight into some realm of mystery and mystical ecstacy, but rather that the reality of authentic existence cannot be obscured even by the empirical structure of human contingency. Instead of contradicting empirical existence, being "in Jesus Christ" asserts it by transfiguring it. And thus the Christ-event, like the creation, is for Calvin the ground upon which the concretion of man's metaphysical rebellion against any kind of reductionism is not only possible but also real. There is here no question of some sort of a "leap of faith," except if it is clearly understood that this leap is already taken with the assumption itself of one's contingency as a parable of the givenness of God's reality of which the creation and the Christ-event are the *sacraments,* i.e., the "worldliness" of God's reality of which the human reality can be the "experience," the actuality.[13] Being himself what God does, Jesus Christ represents and makes present again what God does to save man. Jesus Christ is the "secularization" of God's faithfulness to man. And because the Christ-event is thus God's own secularity, the secular itself is not rejected but asserted as the legitimate dimension of eschatological existence. Or, as Calvin would say, Christ is the "hand" by which self-knowledge is led to the knowledge of God.

But, it will be asked, what of the idea that "the knowledge of God is naturally rooted in the spirit of man," that innate in man is an ineradicable awareness of divinity?[14] The answer is: both general revelation and the *sensum divinitatis* play one and the same role: God is revealed in nature and in history and we would see it if the question, not of God, but of man were naturally possible without contradicting itself, if self-knowledge were autonomous, or simply if we had faith. It follows, then, that man is infinitely without excuse, and is equally without excuse when he takes God for granted and *ipso facto* worships an idol. Thus, in order "to prevent anyone from taking refuge in the pretense of ignorance," Calvin writes, "God himself has implanted in all men a certain understanding of his divine majesty. Ever renewing its memory, he repeatedly sheds fresh drops. Since, therefore, men one and all perceive that there is a

God and that he is their Maker (*il nous a formez*), they are condemned by their own testimony. . . ."[15]

Thus the idea of the innateness of God in man, rather than being a loop-hole that would allow man to hedge around his own incoherence, forces him to face it inescapably and to accept it without consenting to it, even as faith takes up doubt without consenting to it. God is no cog in any self-explanatory system of existence. Against those who fancy "that divinity [is] poured out into the various parts of the world," Calvin argues that surely God's "infinity ought to make us afraid to try to measure him by our senses" even though being "incomprehensible he also fills the earth itself."[16] Despite certain aspects in Calvin's reasoning which seem to indicate the contrary, God is not an existential hypothesis. Calvin's stress on the necessity to differentiate God from idols is his own way of making the same point.

In keeping with the traditional language of theology, he articulates his views in terms of the doctrine of the Trinity. First, as Niesel points out, "the doctrine of the Trinity secures the unity of God by distinguishing him from idols."[17] Second, the doctrine of the Trinity further discriminates faith from esoteric speculative knowledge by establishing at once the verbal nature of reality and the empirical character of the Word of God: the creation itself as revelatory of the divine reality is a sacrament of which the Christ-event is the Word.[18] Or else why does Moses, Calvin argues, "expressly tell us that God in his individual acts of creation spoke, Let this or that be done [Gen. 1] unless so that the unsearchable glory of God may shine forth in his image?" And in the fourth Gospel,

> John spoke most clearly of all when he declared that that Word, God, from the beginning with God, was at the same time the cause of all things. . . . Therefore, inasmuch as all divinely uttered revelations are correctly designated by the term "Word of God," so this substantial Word is properly placed at the highest level, as the wellspring of all oracles. Unchangeably, the Word abides everlastingly one and the same with God, and is God himself.[19]

Third, by ensuring historical existence as the proper arena of faith, and by focusing faith on Christ, the doctrine of the Trinity echoes the New Testament's convictions that what distinguishes God from the idols is the Christ-event and that, though faith is the principal work of the Spirit,[20] it is nonetheless "in the flesh" that man encounters the God who is a Spirit: "There, indeed, does the pious mind perceive the very presence of God, and almost touches him, when it feels quickened, illumined, preserved, justified, and sanctified."[21]

No wonder, then, that Calvin insists on the sovereignty or the honor and majesty of God. Nor is it surprising that he should be consistent with the logic of faith, and develop the much derided doctrine of predestination. Indeed, natural man is, for Calvin, neither adamic man nor fallen man; natural man is predestined man, inasmuch as "natural" cannot mean autonomous, even less heteronomous, except by virtue of an optical illusion.

Because Calvin's perspective on the notion of God is commanded by the question *Qualis sit Deus?* and not *Quid sit Deus?* it follows that the concept of God's sovereignty should be closely allied with that of his redemptive activity in Christ, or else "sovereignty" would hardly have meant anything different from man in capital letters, and God would be omnipotent or omniscient simply because man is not. Calvin does not care about such attributes of God. They are not "expedient" for the knowledge of faith. The sovereignty of God simply means that when God saves he really saves, he really has the power to save. And he saves regardless of man's demerits as well as of his merits. In other words, God has the power to predestine.

This is not the place to go into all the details of the doctrine of predestination and its antecedents in the Fathers and in the Bible. Basically, Calvin is in agreement with Augustine, for whom, as Thomas Aquinas points out, "predestination is a work aimed at showing mercy," a doctrine which deals with "the destination of one who is."[22] For Aquinas himself, "predestination is not anything in the predestined, but only in the person who predestines."[23] Even so, predestination makes no sense if one should overlook what might be called its Christological axis, if it does not focus upon the Christ-event. For, as Calvin writes in a passage of *The Eternal Predestination of God* where he cites Augustine, "no more glorious glass, in which to behold predestination, exists than the blessed Mediator himself, who according to his human nature, considered as such, attained to the honour of becoming the only begotten Son of God by no merit of his own."[24] Nor can the dignity of man, Calvin argues in the *Institutes,* be determined by his good works as though it could be derived from some source other than God:[25] man's only dignity "lies in God's freely given love,"[26] by virtue of which "election has as its goal holiness of life,"[27] namely, faith as eschatological existence, i.e., authentic existence here and now. Not only is thus predestination directed against the theory of good works, it is also meant to question the claim that empirical reality is in and of itself hostile or simply that it can be used as a speculative ground for reducing the human experience to some sophisticated form of philosophical determinism, to the secularistic notion of fate.

Declaring "how offensive to [him] is the profane term fate,"[28] Calvin argues that it is "a term given by Stoics to their doctrine of necessity, which they had formed out of a multiplex labyrinth of contradictory reasonings; a doctrine calculated to call God himself to order, and to set him laws whereby to work. But predestination I define to be, according to the Holy Scriptures, that free and unfettered counsel of God by which he rules all men and things, and also all parts and particles of the world by his infinite wisdom and incomprehensible justice."[29] Over against fate or determinism which, so to speak, conflates in an immanentist way the reality of God with the reality of man, Calvin's point is that while the reality of God is the possibility of human existence, it is nevertheless given with the fact of existence; that is why, although he holds that election is, symbolically speaking, "anterior" to faith (pre-destination), it can, however, only be grasped in faith, or through faith;[30] but, then, faith is the expression of this grasping.

Predestination thus harks back to God's sovereignty which itself harks back to God's redemptive activity in the Christ-event. That is to say, salvation is not a past occurrence, but a present reality. God *constantly* saves man. And, if so, God's decision to save man can never be affected by man's subsequent way of life: man is saved in spite of his goodness as well as because of his sinfulnes. The prefix "pre" refers, so to speak, not to some sort of chronological antecedence of God,[31] but to God's eschatological antecedence, to the identity between the Alpha and the Omega, between the God who was and is and ever shall be and the God who comes, and of whom Christ is the mirror. And in Christ, despite my sinfulness, despite even my faith which is lack of faith and is in constant need of prodding, my destination is now the existence I can invent, the freedom with which the present is invested by the future.

Nor is destiny—or eschatological existence—to be identified with morality, with human standards of behavior. No wonder Calvin called predestination both a terrible decree (for it nullifies our pretensions) and a "sweet"[32] doctrine (for we need no longer pretend but simply be). Indeed, existence is now endowed with its *original* meaning and purpose (by which is not meant a pre-established pattern, but one that is not predetermined by the past). From this point of view, Calvin's concept of vocation, so different from both Luther's and Aquinas's, is expressive of the necessity to assume secularity as the sphere of man's loyalty to God, of the freedom of faith. Involvement in the world is, indeed, the necessary corollary of commitment to God. For if the world to come has any meaning, it must begin by rooting itself in this world, by assuming the form of this world. Such is, *per vocationem,* the nature of man's responsibility.[33] Only the free man can assume it. Otherwise he would be without excuse, and condemned even by his innate sense of divinity.

## 2-B

Our interpretation of Calvin's theology may be summed up in the following way: The sense of divinity corresponds to the concept of God as creator; vocation, with its infrastructure in the notion of total depravity and its suprastructure in that of holiness of life, corresponds to God as redeemer; and to God as fulfiller ("the one who predestines") corresponds the twin concept of freedom and responsibility. The world is the theater of God's glory, and the chief end of man is to glorify God. What remains now to be done is to assess Calvin's method in order to ensure the discussion of norms and criteria with which the third part of this chapter will deal more specifically.

The first remark about Calvin's method is so obvious that it scarcely needs to be mentioned. The *Institutes,* to take his dogmatic *magnum opus,* is much less systematic than, say, Tillich's *Systematic Theology*. In fact, philosophically speaking, it is not systematic at all. For all its platonist residue it still does not subscribe to any single fundamental philosophical premise. And while it may be said that *cur deus homo* is its theme, this *deus* is no philosophical principle but the God of Abraham, of Jacob, of Isaac, who in Christ encounters man and reconciles the world unto himself.

Second, even the innateness of God is not some kind of pre-Tillichian ultimate concern later to be identified with God. Though God "sowed in men's mind that seed of religion . . ."[34] nothing prevents man from idolatry; on the contrary, idolatry abounds. In other words, the innateness of God is no principle according to which it could be claimed that reason calls for revelation. Rather, we are tempted to say, Calvin would hold that it is revelation which calls for reason. And only in this sense could one legitimately detect and speak of a certain method of correlation—a correlation, furthermore, which does not justify but is justified by the Christ-event.

Nor is it a question, to put it differently, whether the soul is *naturaliter christiana;* instead, it would seem that Calvin is concerned rather with the question, what kind of man is *spiritualiter humanus.* Thus, no more than he really begins with the hypothesis of God, does he assume the idea of a human nature prior to individual man, of an essence prior to existence. In another but not unrelated context, Calvin himself writes: "Therefore we declare that man is corrupted through natural vitiation, but a vitiation that did not flow from nature. We deny that it has flowed from nature in order to indicate that it is an adventitious quality which comes upon man rather than a substantial property which has been implanted from the beginning."[35]

Third, Calvin's theology does not, so to speak, develop the proposition that the question of man leads to the question of God. On the contrary, it is the question of God which leads to the question of man, for the simple reason, Calvin contends, that "everyone can always find in his fantasy some sort of superstition: man's brain (I say) is like an idolatry shop: let there be no master and everyone will make up some idol, everyone will pervert the service of God."[36]

Finally, the reality of the Church is not set up against that of the world. But the Church is the transfiguration of the world; the Church is where the world recovers its original integrity. The universe thus has no self-sustaining purpose, but is the arena of God's creative and redemptive design, the glory of God. The reality of the Church is accordingly secular as well as spiritual. It is a world-facing, world-honoring and world-assuming reality. Thus conceived, Calvin's understanding of the nature of the Church may be described as centrifugal and replaces the centripetal conception of the Middle Ages. It would not be illegitimate here to paraphrase the dictum, according to which *novum testamentum in vetere latet, vetus in novo patet,* by saying: *ecclesia in mundo latet, mundum in ecclesia patet.* From such a perspective, one might even argue, is Calvin's design for Geneva to be appreciated. Indeed, just as we cannot imagine the Christian faith without a cultural dimension, so we cannot conceive of the *communio sanctorum* without a social and political dimension.

## 3

So far so good. But how can one do theology in a post-Christian era? What of the death of God, that cultural phenomenon in terms of which we, today, must abide by the rule of methodological atheism? Does it not cut us off from the tradition of the Christian faith and its source?

Our definition of the post-Christian implies in effect that a new theological method must be inaugurated in order to take into account both our commitment to the Christian faith and our involvement in the present world. It is precisely in this respect that we find Calvin's work most helpful and relevant in more ways than one, excepting of course blind appeal and unexamined subservience to it. (As he himself would have said, in every theology some doctrines are more important than others.)

Divided into four books, the plan of the *Institutes* has often been described as adhering to the four articles of the Creed. To be sure, there is something arbitrary about this similarity; other articulations of the *Institutes* have been suggested that do more justice to the logic of Calvin's argument. But this is of secondary importance. What I should like to stress is that the four books of the *Institutes* do give us the four marks of theology for today. These marks are indicative of our commitment to the Christian faith and its tradition; they are also the key with which to unlock the cipher of our post-Christian culture. The four marks are these:

First, knowledge is theonomous. That is to say, there is a correlation between the question of God and the question of man. More precisely, theology is that kind of concrete science which holds that, even on empirical grounds, the question of man cannot be so formulated as to rule out *ipso facto* the question of God. When Calvin contends that the latter makes the former possible, we understand him to mean that they are not identical; that neither obliterates the other; that if the present immanentist worldview prohibits any theistic premise, it also prevents conceiving of faith as a prolongation of some aspect of human nature; and that, correspondingly, biblical thought conceives of eschatological existence not as an extension of the flesh but as its transfiguration. Hence the real question is not: How can one believe? The question is: How can one not believe? As Faulkner would say: "How can a man be expected to know even enough to doubt?"[37] Or Calvin: "Unbelief is, in all men, always mixed with faith."[38] In other words, man's natural, empirical, understanding of himself cannot without canceling itself at the same time, cancel the knowledge of faith. Man always seeks an Unknown God. Yet God always seeks man.

Second, theology is Christological. That is, there is no other God than he who is accessible through Christ alone: God is neither here nor there. Should we look for him even in Christ, we should only find a man. God cannot be found at the expense of man. He has no reality if it does not assert that of man. Nor can the latter be affirmed except through faith, here and now. And if today's radical immanentism is a sign that modern man is tired of otherworldly delusions and of frustrated expectations, the Christ-event is, according to Calvin, the sign that these have been vanquished. Indeed, the Christian must not merely put up with this world; he must affirm its original goodness, for eschatological existence precisely means that there is no other world than this one in which to have faith and live.[39]

Third, theology is pneumatic. That is, it lacks philosophical presuppositions; more accurately it is not wedded to them. And the reason for this is that, somehow, every philosophy conceals a self-proving theology—the very opposite of a theology springing from the Word of God. And yet, because it is pneumatic, theology assumes the very categories of our understanding. Calvin's theology seems systematic. It is not. It seems to adopt a particular worldview, but does not capitulate to it.[40]

Fourth, theology is ecclesiastical. That is, it is historical, cultural, political: it is worldly. It is not determined by this or that cultural stance, this or that historical factor, this or that political axis. But theology fails if it does not assume them.

In other words, the task of the theologian is to articulate the faith in spite of its past creedal or dogmatic statements. The Word of God is to be believed in spite of the Bible. Though the Bible is written in the language of a theonomous or transcendental frame of reference, the Word of God is not necessarily bound to it.

But the more post-Christian a theologian is, the more he will turn to the tradition of the Christian era, remembering that no worldview is scientifically better than a previous one, but is simply more expedient. And expediency should not delude him into thinking that our contemporaries understand themselves better than Paul understood himself, or Augustine, or Thomas, or Calvin.

The real problem is not whether we should lean on Heidegger, or Marx, or Whitehead, or Eliade, or whether we should—because God is dead—develop some principle of cross-fertilization by seeking help from Buddhism. Eastern or Western pre-Christian or post-Christian, old-time or avant-garde, it is not religion that saves. The problem is whether the bedridden, paralytic, and tradition-bound theologian will hear Jesus' injunction: Take thy bed and walk.

# The Church, the World, and Ethics

And behold, one came up to him, saying, "Teacher, what good deed must I do, to have eternal life?" And he said to him, "Why do you ask me about what is good. If you should enter life, keep the commandments." . . . The young man said to him, "All these I have observed; what do I still lack?" Jesus said to him, "If you would be perfect, go, sell what you possess and give it to the poor, and you will have treasure in heaven; and come, follow me."

(Matt. 19/16–17, 20–21)

# VI

## The Church, the World, and Ethics

At a time when sociology is replacing ecclesiology[1] a further aspect of Christianity's shortcoming becomes evident: ethics makes sense only to the extent of the social relevance of the Church. The question is not simply whether or not ethics must be subsumed under theology, whether or not Christian ethics is "contextual,"[2] or "situational,"[3] or whether it should be pegged on some theory of natural law.[4] As a matter of fact, what these alternatives themselves reveal is that without ecclesiology, i.e., a doctrine whereby the Church is understood as a dimension of the modern world, Christian ethics can only cease to be a live option. By and large, the present moral teaching of the Church only points to the fact that it was relevant as an institution in the past, let us say, in the Middle Ages.

In this light, let us first of all rid ourselves of a few misunderstandings:

1. By claiming that the social ethics of the Bible no longer is valid in a universe where technology has upset our conceptions of man's relationship to the world, what is as-

serted is simply that the cultural framework in which (and thanks to which) this ethics took shape is today superannuated. Indeed, if Bible and Word of God must not be confused it is equally appropriate to distinguish carefully that which in the ethical teaching of the Bible is but the reflection of a certain natural cultural will—the social consciousness of which, though it was perhaps determined in terms of divine revelation, was nevertheless legitimatized by a conception of the world—and an image of man commensurate with this will. The conflict, or simply the lag we deplore between Christianity and the contemporary world, comes from the fact that the political and social involvement of the Church is not legitimatized by the master ideas of our period, nor is it supported by the goals implicit in our way of understanding the world today and of projecting the human adventure.

2. One can say of the Bible that it provides us with social teachings or with principles and values "for all times" only to the extent that these teachings, principles and values are frankly tributary of the cultural and social framework in whose terms they are enunciated. Unless this tributary character is recognized, "for all times" could only mean a surcease disloyally granted on Sunday at eleven o'clock to the universe of Ptolemy, to the Roman Empire, to the dialect of Canaan; the result of which is not, as one would be tempted to think, to underline the tributary aspect that I have just mentioned but to congeal divine revelation and make it depend upon certain conditions without which it would not be possible and could have no effect. And that would indeed be the surest way of turning the Church into its own caricature, a survival of the past. And yet there, more than anywhere else, faith should demonstrate its worldliness, its secularity. Not from the world is the Christian faith to be preserved but from its own loss of flavor, from its transformation into a kind of computer providing ready-made answers to questions we have survived.

3. If then the Bible itself, its social teachings, its ethical

principles and its moral values are partly the expression of a cultural phenomenon it is not surprising that in this respect, too, Christianity has just completed a page of its history, that of the Constantinian period or "Christian" era. This page we have no other choice but to turn, and we wish to turn it only because we believe that the Bible can still provide us with a social ethics attuned to our situation.

4. Finally, we must dissipate a misunderstanding which deals with the so-called Christian civilization. Against the despisers of Christianity one must have the candor to assert both the amplitude and originality of the successes won by Christianity as a cultural ferment in the field of political action as well as in shaping the type of humanism which is characteristic of Western culture. On the other hand, we must also snatch from the nostalgic adepts their illusions of Christian civilization as the golden age of the West, and bring them to recognize that the cultural triumph of Christianity does not make its cultural vocation or obligation dependent on the institutions we have inherited.

## 1

On the basis of these clarifications it is easy to realize that the validity of biblical exegesis and theology hinges on the threefold necessity of disengaging the biblical message from the political and philosophical concepts to which it was linked, of emancipating us from them, and of preparing for the biblical message new avenues to the political and social scene of today's world. After all, what must be deplored is not the way in which the Church understood in the past the task of its obligation to secularity so much as the contention that that way is the only way. From such a contention nothing is gained other than the falsification of the biblical message, whose concrete characteristic is that it must remain at once bound to the contingencies of the world and be independent of them.

That is why an ethics which would be centered on the

chief problem of today, namely the problem of God, will be all the more Christian in that it will not be subservient to our traditional moral values. Our situation is like that of the rich young man (Matt. 19/16–21) or like the situation of those who were shocked by Jesus when he declared to them that it was the Sabbath that was made for man, not man for the Sabbath. In other words, we keep thinking of ethics as consisting of do's and don'ts, as if the question "what ought I to do?" could be validly raised apart from the question of God, that is, apart from the context of the Church as the reality of God's worldliness.

Part of our ethical dilemma today stems not from the impossibility of a sound theological ethics but from the fact that such ethics is deprived of the context in which to operate meaningfully. Equally a part of this dilemma is our traditional conception of ethics as a system of predicting human conduct, as if losing one's self in order to gain it could at all be codified. Accordingly, to advocate or to be shocked by the "new morality" scarcely faces the problem, certain aspects of which deal with the fact that if modern man has become emancipated from the Christian ethic this is because Christian thought has not been able to emancipate itself from its bondage to sclerotic concepts, to liquidate its own past in order to assume the obligations of the present time. In the sixteenth century Calvin, for example, did not hesitate to bring his caution to usury, and surely one cannot say that it was the theological tradition that prompted him to it. Quite the contrary. In acting thus Calvin definitely showed that theology does not have among its tasks that of defending the *status quo ante* as regards economics any more than as regards faith itself.

Theology today is lagging behind the options we must face in the domain of social ethics. Perhaps the rapidity with which these options overtake us and the urgency of the decisions we must make will demand, if they have not already done so, that theology start *de novo* so that it may run with the wind without becoming a weather vane and without denying its specific vocation. Meanwhile, in order to meet the slackness of theology we must satisfy ourselves with occasional *ad hoc* options for want of a global ethic. The dilemma simply is that we have the theology our civilization deserves, or rather we do not have the theology, much less the ecclesiology and ethic, our world deserves. Hence we must improvise. And we must improvise in such a way that at least our actions may speak for a faith that otherwise has become speechless.

The task is not easy. Let those who might think otherwise reflect on, for instance, the Protestant ethic which, what with the turn that capitalism took by dehumanizing work and by cutting off man's moral involvement in the world from his commitment to God (business is business), sank into a reassuring formalism, and thus further stressed the cleavage between the Church and the world, between the Christian faith and modern man.

More than ever we have therefore the salutary occasion to realize that it is not the world which is made for the Church but the Church for the world. And we begin to grasp this occasion if, consciously or not, we do not transform the Christian faith into an ethico-social particularism. Such a particularism, even if one can consider it as having been the guarantee of the cultural and social vocation that the Church exercised for centuries, would today result in the conversion of the Church into a ghetto, and Church membership into a matter of private custom. This would no doubt be the easiest solution. But it would corroborate the demise of the Church.

To yield to the temptation exerted upon us by the cultural obsolescence of Christianity, as well as by the technological mentality for which moral problems tend to become equations to solve, would amount to acquiescing to the neutralization of the Christian tradition as a cultural ferment. But to sterilize the Christian faith would deviate the biblical message from its field of action—the world. Even if the precedent of apostolic times was claimed, by doing so the Church would not only constitute itself as an enclave off the mainstream of contemporary society but would also deceive itself into believing that the situation of the early Christians could be repeated. The circumstances are no longer the same, nor must one be isolated from the world in order not to conform to it.

Today's world, by contrast with that of the apostles, is the beneficiary of the impact of the Christian faith on its human as well as cultural and social structures. As a matter of fact, it is in connection with these structures that one can follow the progressive development by which the spirit of secularity fostered by Christianity was being degraded into its opposite, secularism. Thus the refusal of heteronomy (in particular the kind of heteronomy which the Christian tradition has unfortunately come to signify and incarnate), and the desire to overcome the alienation that the Christian ethic represents today, have expressed themselves by a drive toward the double illusion of a radical autonomy which cannot project itself without destroying itself and of an innocence which cannot be lived without guilt. While the universe of absolute transcendence was being leveled down in order to give way to a world where radical immanentism reigns, existence has undergone the metamorphosis from an act of faith to an exercise in self-assertion without a mandate. A new religiosity has thus come about, which must be taken into account, and on its own terms.

On the other hand, the legacy of Christianity does not consist of the death of God only. It also includes the vast number of functions and responsibilities which once were ecclesiastical and have become public or governmental, or even private. Though largely de-Christianized, the world in which we live may not be after all as evil as that of the Apostles. Exactly this is what in fact makes our job at once easier and more difficult. Easier, because we should at least in theory be able to speak the same language as our contemporaries. But also more difficult, because today's paganism is "Christian." As the index of the erosion of the spirituality of Christian culture, this new mentality gives no hold to the Christian faith, much less when it is proclaimed through its traditional channels.

## 2

It is *qua* social ideology that the Church has been overtaken by the dominant models of contemporary thought. I would go so far as to say that the similar resignation to technocratic efficiency on the part of otherwise antagonistic political ideologies is itself also a repercussion of the dishabilitation of Christianity as an ideological ferment.

Be that as it may, and regardless of what one may say theologically, it is nevertheless in terms of specific social data that the idea of the Church took flesh, and these data no longer correspond to ours. In other words, it is the very notion of the Church that must be re-examined if we do not intend to shortchange the human person by saddling him with a social ethic that would at best be irrelevant to the problems of contemporary society. Indeed, what is a human person? Every possible definition shows that being a member of the Church has nothing to do with it.

Is a human person, for example, the French woman whom the organizers of a certain domestic arts exhibit in Paris wanted to convince that all the magnificent appliances displayed were now within the reach of every French woman? This in spite of the fact that most women in France cannot afford to buy these appliances, or, when they can, have no place to put them in those thousands of new apartments where kitchens are conceived without any space left for even a refrigerator; not to mention the problems involved in using these appliances with inadequate electric wiring or water pipes. Or is the human person the American woman whose existence is inundated with gadgets and finds no time to do anything? Or is it the Mennonite woman who turns her back on the world in order to live according to the fashion of her ancestors? These three rudimentary cases indicate that sooner or later one must come to grips with registering a certain demise of the Church as a social body, whereas in the past it created our universities and hospitals, and so on. When it comes to the welfare of the human being the Church still lives in the time of good works, while the state and its technocrats develop Social Security, Medicare, etc. However one feels about it today, medieval Christendom had at least the merit of promulgating the theory of the Three Estates.

This does not mean that Christianity as a whole is now completely cut off from the world. It still has a few possibilities of action, which have been attempted not without success. If in this century of transition the Church cannot legitimately claim to be able to formulate a social ethic or even a coherent global theology, its members nevertheless can still act, and provided they are involved in the world without restriction their action can have, and has already proved that it can have, as much efficacy on the practical level as the social theories of the Middle Ages did. It is only on the basis of such initiatives that one can legitimately hope to see the beginnings of new forms of thought that will necessarily affect the structures of the Church as much as the style of its cultural, political, and social vocation. If to our greatest shame we must recognize that it is not the Church but the state which in the United States has been the avant-garde in the fight for racial equality, one must also underline that it is in part the direct action taken outside of the Church by individual Christians that triggered the measures adopted by the Supreme Court. Even if the Church can only follow and align itself, it will end ultimately by not only admitting but also fashioning the new visage of a Christianity adapted to the political, social, intellectual, and cultural structures of our time.

It goes without saying that only particular circumstances can dictate the style of the Christian's political involvement and, depending on the case, this involvement will take place on the professional level or will emanate from movements like[5] "Christianity and Crisis." Nor is this to be construed as advocating a thoroughgoing subjectivism or ethical occasionalism. They can both be avoided if such involvements are also accompained by a complete reconversion of ecclesiology. Nor have the social tasks of the Church been exhausted. They seem to be, of course, only when the Church can condone tasteless bread and at the same time wonder why communion has become meaningless. Christians ought to learn something from the rabbinical supervision of kosher foods.

In other words, one should not lament the fact that others, such as the state or private foundations have today assumed the great cultural, political, and social tasks that the Church in the past initiated and accomplished, and from which our civilization benefited before turning its back on Christianity. The essential thing today is that Christianity should not miss its vocation by not assuming even the humblest tasks to which its adherents may be brought in spite of their faithfulness to the Church. As in the parable of the last judgment, could it not be that these were the most urgent and decisive tasks? And could it not be that their style is the one that behooves the Church's involvement in the world?

# Appendix

THE FOLLOWING is meant to clarify the issues with which the various essays of this book are concerned in one form or another.

## I. The Christian Era

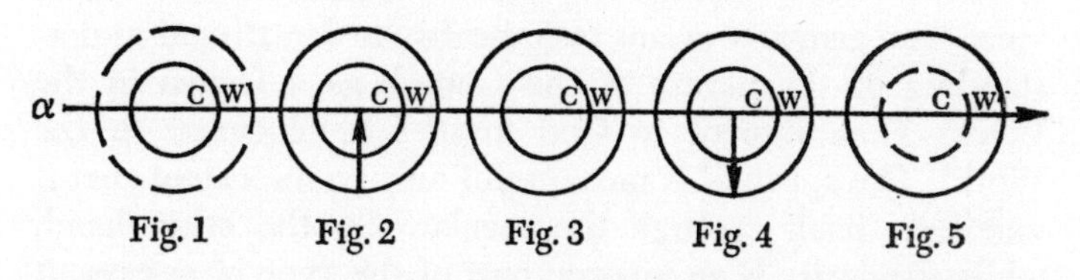


(C = the Church; W = the World)

Based largely upon Richard Niebuhr's study of the various ways in which the relevance of the Christian faith to culture has been understood throughout history (*Christ and Culture*, New York, Harper and Brothers, 1951), the legend for the above diagrams may thus be stated:

1. *Christ against culture:* This view is the answer to those who, from Tertullian to the Amish, have advocated not only renouncing the World in order not to conform to it, but also withdrawing from it. Such a view is predicated on a necessary antagonism between the Church and the World.

2. *Christ above culture:* This view primarily is the answer of the medieval synthesis as reflected both in the hierarchical conceptuality of Thomas Aquinas and in the sacramentarian understanding of life whether secular or religious.

The arrow is meant to indicate the centripetal organization of the World around the Church (which is also reflected in the conviction that reason leads to revelation) as well as the sacerdotal view that nature is not destroyed but assumed by grace.

3. *Christ and culture in paradox:* One might say for the sake of simplicity that this is the view of the Lutheran Reformation. The Church and the World must be distinguished but not separated just as a difference is to be maintained between the public and the private sectors, even to the extent, as Luther said, that a prince must govern as a prince and not as a Christian. Thus the important thing here is not the conflict between the Church and the World but the conflict between God and man.

4. *Christ the transformer of culture:* This is the Calvinistic view. The arrow is meant to indicate the centrifugal understanding of the nature of the Church as a leaven in the World. Commitment to God implies involvement in the World. The spiritual is meaningful only to the extent that it manifests itself through the secular. On the other hand, while secularity is an integral part of this type of answer, it has not been altogether able to avoid secularism.

5. *The Christ of culture:* This is the view of those who throughout the ages have sought primarily to accommodate faith with the exigencies of the cultural situation even to the point of surrender.

## II. The Post-Christian Era

All the above five types have one thing in common. However the diagram is construed, the Church is, for all practical purposes, more or less conceived as a society *within* society, almost geographically as well as sociologically distinct from the World, the profane (*pro-fanum*—that which is before the Temple). Such an understanding of the Church is tributary of the general worldview of the Christian era. Part of our problem is that today the structures of the Church as well as the patterns of theological thinking reflect the concerns of that era and are not adapted to the mentality of modern man.

The emergence of a post-Christian era makes it all the more imperative not only to rethink theology on the basis of a new model but also to recast the structures of the Church in terms of man's personal and social self-understanding today. A mobile and dynamic society has replaced the traditional stable structures in the light of which the nature of the Church was construed. In a post-Christian age the Church cannot remain at the center of the village if it wants to be present in the midst of life. Nor can it resort to becoming an enclave, a modernistic ghetto. Much less can Christianity forfeit itself by becoming merely a private matter. And inasmuch as all of the five types somehow imply that, so to speak, the Church is one side of the coin of which the other is the World, it would seem that unless Christianity wants to be wiped off the face of the earth, the Church must begin to think of itself not as a place of retreat from the world, not as a society within society, but as a community that has no reality other than *through* the society of men, as the avant-garde of society, as the axis of culture.

That, *mutatis mutandis,* the Church played such a role in the past is testified by the various ecclesiastical functions now taken over by the state (e.g., schools and hospitals). Instead of wondering what would be left for the Church to do should the state continue to infringe on the attributes of the Church and should sociology replace ecclesiology, Christians need to come to grips with the fact that there are always new things to do though they may not much resemble, at least superficially, those tasks the Church undertook in the past. Among other things, theology will have to enter the fields of, e.g., literature, politics, and economics, if it wants to tackle the chief problem of our age, namely, the problem of God. Otherwise, it will merely engage in the business of updating the Church. And that is not the position to take, especially if being the Church means also being the avant-garde of society, the axis of culture, the strategy for which may be conveyed by the following diagram:

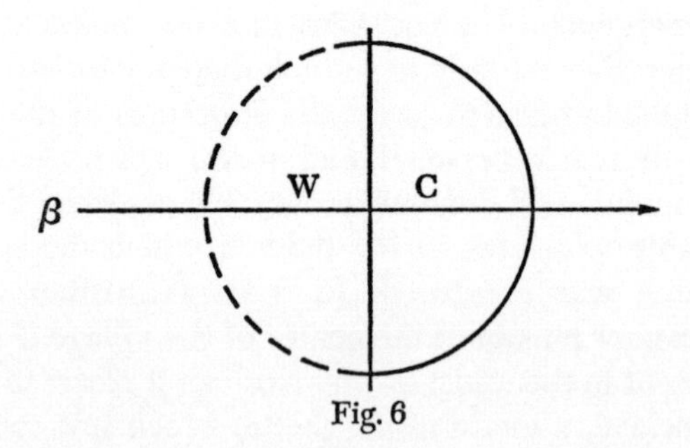


Fig. 6

## III. The Death of God as a Cultural Phenomenon

Figures 7a and 7b are meant to carry the same idea, that of the death of God as a cultural phenomenon. The point is that in the Christian era ($\alpha$) man ($C_1$) understands himself in the context of $B_1$ (let us say, his worldview) and in terms of $A_1$ (God). The reason for distinguishing $A_1$ and $B_1$ is that even from the traditional point of view God ($A_1$) was not merely an adjunct of a particular worldview ($B_1$). The shift from $\alpha$ to $\beta$, expressive of the leveling-down from radical monotheism to radical immanentism suggests that post-Christian man (whether he be a Christian or not) lives at $C_2$. The death of God is the name for that phenomenon which takes place when:

a) $\beta$-man ($C_2$) confines his self-understanding in terms of today's scientific and technological worldview ($\beta_2$) and erects its empirically based methodological atheism into an ideology according to which he claims that since $A_1$ (God) cannot make sense at $\beta$ he is dead [$C_2B_2A_1$];

b) a Christian lives at $B_2$ and claims he understands himself as $C_1$ in terms of $A_1$ [$A_1B_2C_1$];

c) today's Christian ($C_2$) accommodating $B_1$ to $B_2$ or $B_2$ to $B_1$ hopes thereby to preserve the reality of $A_1$,

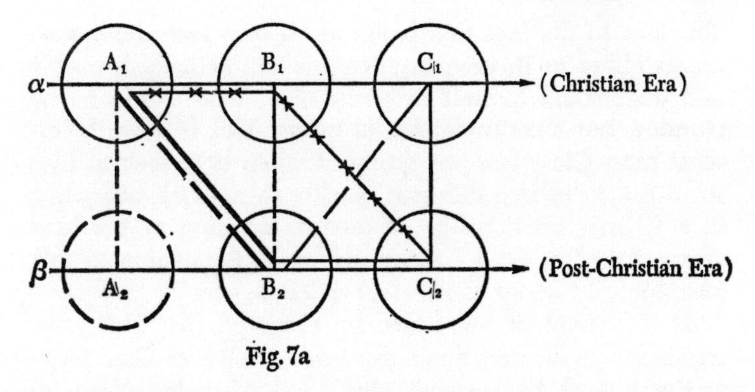


Fig. 7a

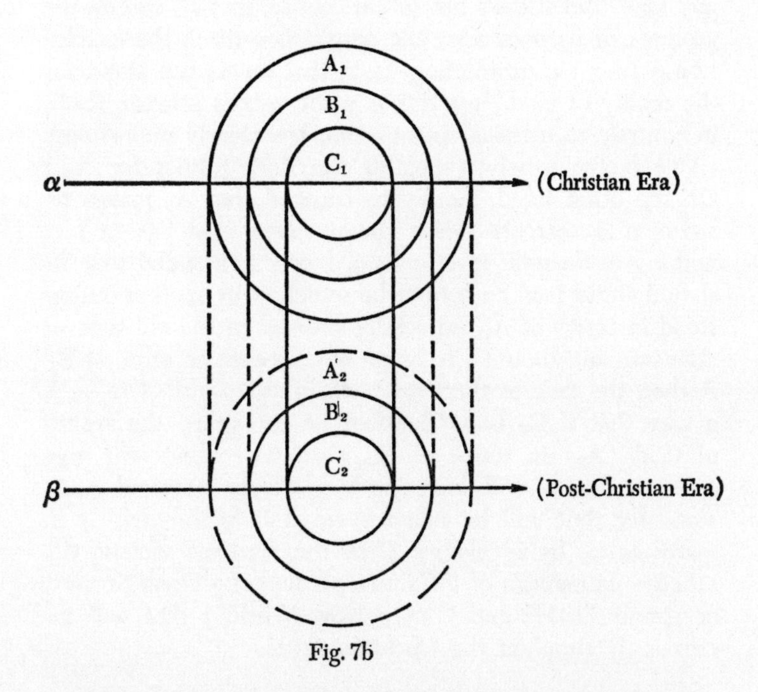


Fig. 7b

The vertical lines of Figures 7a and 7b mean that the shift from $\alpha$ to $\beta$ has taken place ($C_1$ $C_2$), or that it has taken place by default (of $B_1$ in the case of $B_1$ $B_2$), or that $A_2$ does and does not correspond to $A_1$.

oblivious to the fact that being at $C_1$ *ipso facto* he has no access either to $B_1$ or to $A_1$. No one can actually live at $\beta$ and understand himself in terms of $\alpha$. That would be no paradox, but a contradiction in terms. This is nevertheless what most Christians are guilty of when they seek to live, so to speak, in two different worlds ($\alpha$ and $\beta$), according to a $C_2B_1A_1$ relationship, instead of working at the kind of reconversion ($B_2$) that would make it possible to talk meaningfully about God ($A_2$) [$C_2B_1A_1$].

At this point, it must also be observed that if $B_1$ was somehow predicated upon the prior reality of God ($A_1$), at the $\beta$ level, by contrast, God ($A_2$) is no hypothesis of any kind. But it does not follow, either, that $B_2$ can on the grounds of its own scientific empiricism reach the conclusion, without contradicting itself, that no $A_2$ can stand for the reality of God. Just this is what today's atheism itself, in contrast to classical anti-theism, has clearly understood. (This factor is what explains the dotted lines for $A_2$.) On the other hand, simply to contend that $A_1$ makes no sense at $\beta$ scarcely meets the problem, and has in fact nothing to do with it. Nor have I ever contended that $B_2$ should either lead back to or be somehow or another understood in terms of $A_1$, especially since even the old type of atheism (anti-theism), to begin with, makes no sense at $B_2$. Rather, the task of theology is to grapple with $\beta$ in such a way that if $C_2$ is a Christian he can grasp the reality of God ($A_2$) in terms of $B_2$. Otherwise what will give meaning to $A_2$ will have nothing to do with what $A_1$ stood for, but will be taken over, as it legitimately is in many cases, by ideologies (like the classless society, the atheistic humanism of a Camus, perhaps the Great Society, or simply "1984" and "Brave New World") that will increasingly supplant the Christian faith.

# References

## I. The Poverty of Theology

1. Rudolf Bultmann, "The Idea of God and Modern Man," *Journal for Theology and the Church,* vol. 2 (New York, Harper Torchbooks, 1965), pp. 83–95; F. Thomas Trotter, "Variations on the 'Death of God' Theme in Recent Theology," *The Journal of Bible and Religion* 38 (1965), 1, 42–48.
2. In particular, Thomas J. J. Altizer and William Hamilton whose collected essays, *Radical Theology and the Death of God* were published in 1966 (New York, Bobbs-Merrill).

## II. The End of the Age of Religion?

1. Rudolf Bultmann, "New Testament and Mythology," *Kerygma and Myth,* edited by Hans Werner Bartsch and translated by R. H. Fuller (London, S.P.C.K., 1953); *Jesus Christ and Mythology* (New York, Scribners, 1958). The contrast between mythological and scientific thought, needless to say, implies no value judgment. Nor is the myth an invitation to turn one's back on reality, for the sake of a flight into the imaginary. Cf. Claude Lévi-Strauss, *La Pensée sauvage* (Paris, Plon, 1962), p. 25.
2. E.g., Dietrich Bonhoeffer, *Letters and Papers from Prison* (New York, Macmillan Paperbacks, 1962), p. 162: "We are proceeding towards a time of no religion at all: men as they are now simply cannot be religious any more." Somewhat more accurately, though with a different concern, Feuerbach had written: "What yesterday was still religion is no longer such to-day; and what today is atheism, to-

morrow will be religion" (*The Essence of Christianity,* New York, Harper Torchbooks, 1957, p. 32).

3. Thus, when Bonhoeffer writes: "The Church stands not where human powers give out, on the borders, but in the centre of the village" (*op. cit.,* p. 166), it seems to me that, to say the least, he falls back on the wrong argument, indeed, to support his case. Is not exactly this the geographic and centripetal, basically medieval, idea of the Church in the center of the village to which the priest workers ultimately if implicitly objected? Indeed, such a view of the Church can only make sense in a stable society, like the medieval, in which what interests man *"ce n'est pas ce qui bouge, c'est ce qui est stable. Ce qu'ils cherchent, c'est le repos: quies."* (Jacques Le Goff, *La Civilisation de l'occident médiéval,* Paris, Arthaud, 1964, p. 256.)
4. For an unusual book in which the atheistic position does not degenerate into parochial antitheism, cf. Francis Jeanson, *La Foi d'un incroyant* (Paris, Editions du Seuil, 1963). From a similar point of view, John Courtney Murray, S.J., concedes that, indeed, a "pure and most passionate form of atheism, when man rejects God in the name of his own more God-like morality . . . towers high above the petty biblical atheisms and above the shallow monisms of philosophy. Marxist atheism rises toward, if it does not reach, this height of purity and passion." (*The Problem of God,* New Haven and London, Yale University Press, 1964, p. 108.) Cf. also Heinrich Ott, *Theology and Preaching* (Philadelphia, Westminster Press, n.d.), p. 60. Over two centuries ago Pierre Bayle had from an equally theological point of view already argued that atheism and immorality are two different things (*Dictionnaire historique et critique,* art. Lucrèce, Rem. E, K; cf. also *Pensées diverses,* CLXXX and *passim*). By way of contrast, for an example of the kind of atheism that actually dissolves itself into turgid antitheism, cf. Mathias Knuzen's inverted *Credo* in Pierre Bayle, *Dictionnaire historique et critique,* art. Knuzen; equally illuminating is Mgr. Dupanloup's pamphlet *Où allons-nous?* (Paris, Charles Douniol, 1876). Cf. also G. J. Holyoake, *Principles of Secularism* (1859), *The*

*Trial of Theism* (1858), *The Limits of Atheism* (1861), *The Origin and Nature of Secularism* (1896).

5. Bultmann, "The Idea of God and Modern Man," *Journal for Theology and the Church,* Vol. 2, 83–95.
6. Mark 9/24: "I believe, help my unbelief"; Wisd. of Sol. 15/2: "for even if we sin we are thine, knowing thy power. . . ."
7. Bultmann, "The Task of Theology in the Present Situation," *Existence and Faith,* edited and translated by Schubert M. Ogden (New York, Meridian Books, 1960), p. 159: "God is the creator; this means that he is not the cause (α'cτċα) to which thought refers the world, or the source ('αεχή) in terms of which the happenings in the world can be grasped in their unity and lawfulness by the understanding. Rather that God is the Creator means that he encounters us as Lord in our concrete world, in the world that is determined historically, in our actual life in the present." Cf. also Charles N. Cochrane's comments on Augustine's demonology (*Christianity and Classical Culture,* New York, Oxford University Press, 1944, pp. 499–500).
8. Bultmann, *Theology of the New Testament,* II (New York, Scribners, 1955), pp. 73, 76, 86; Ronald Gregor Smith, "Post-Renaissance Man" in Williams Nicholls, ed., *Conflicting Images of Man* (New York, Seabury Press, 1966), pp. 31–49.
9. Bonhoeffer, *op. cit.,* p. 200; Bultmann, "The Idea of God and Modern Man," *op. cit.,* p. 90.
10. For my treatment of the difference between these terms, cf. in particular *The Death of God* (New York, George Braziller, 1961), ch. IV: "Christianity, Secularity and Secularism," and *passim.* On desacralization and secularization as well as secularism cf. also: Augustine, *De civitate dei* XV/7: "And this is the characteristic of the *secular city:* it worships God or gods who might help it reign amidst its victories and over the peace of the earth, not out of any love of coexistence but out of the lust for domination. The good, indeed, use the world in order to enjoy God; but it is in order to enjoy the world that the evil want to use God, provided that, to begin with, they believe

either that God is or that he is concerned with human affairs." (I have translated Augustine's *civitas terrena* by "the secular city"; Cochrane, *op. cit.*, translates it by "secularism.") Cf. also: Le Goff, *op. cit.*, pp. 435–436, 131; Albert Camus, *The Rebel* (New York, Alfred A. Knopf, 1954), *passim.*

11. Bonhoeffer, *op. cit.*, p. 167: "It is not only the mythological conceptions, such as the miracles, the ascension and the like (which are not in principle separable from the conceptions of God, faith and so on) that are problematic, but the 'religious' conceptions themselves." Cf. also p. 164: "How do we speak of God without religion . . . ? How do we speak (but perhaps we are no longer capable of speaking of such things as we used to) in secular fashion of God?" In the light of these quotations and other similar statements, it would seem to me that, at best, as Gerhard Ebeling says, "non-religious interpretation is for Bonhoeffer nothing other than Christological interpretation" (*Word and Faith*, Philadelphia, Fortress Press, 1963, p. 107), unless one is tempted to consider, rather, Bonhoeffer's understanding of Christianity as "a form of practical atheism [which] clothes ordinary liberal forms of life with the romantic unreality of a catacombic vocabulary" (Alasdair MacIntyre, "God and the Theologians," *Encounter* XXI, 3, 1963, p. 9). Cf. also: Ronald Gregor Smith, "A Theological Perspective of the Secular," *The Christian Scholar*, March, 1960, pp. 11–24; André Dumas, "Dietrich Bonhoeffer et l'interprétation du Christianisme comme non-religion," *Archives de Sociologie des religions*, 19 (1965), 5–29; John Godsey, *The Theology of Dietrich Bonhoeffer* (Philadelphia, Westminster Press, 1960); Martin E. Marty, *The Place of Bonhoeffer* (New York, Association Press, 1963); Paul M. Van Buren, *The Secular Meaning of the Gospel* (New York, Macmillan, 1963), pp. xiii, xiv, and *passim.*

12. Cf. Jacques Le Goff, *La Civilisation de l'occident médiéval* (Paris, Arthaud, 1964), pp. 321–325, 336–337, 435. Cf. also M. D. Chenu's remark that "Roland and el Cid, though they are not perfect Christian heroes, exemplify the extent to which religion has pervaded even the brutal-

ity of that bellicose age" (*Saint Thomas d'Aquin et la théologie*, Paris, Ed. du Seuil, 1960, p. 8).

13. Cf. Johann-Baptist Metz, "Unbelief as a Theological Problem," *Concilium* 6 (1965), 59–77, 68–71.
14. I Cor. 4/7: "For who sees anything different in you? What have you that you did not receive? If then you received it, why do you boast as if it were not a gift?" Cf. also Karl Barth, *Christ and Adam* (New York, Harper, 1957), p. 89: " . . . the Christian sphere is not limited to the 'religious' sphere. What is *Christian* is secretly but fundamentally identical with what is *universally human*"; Gérard Philips, "The Church in the Modern World," *Concilium* 6 (1965), 5–22.
15. See Harvey Cox, *The Secular City* (New York, Macmillan, 1965).
16. Bonhoeffer, *op. cit.*, p. 208.
17. Bonhoeffer, *op. cit.*, pp. 219–220.
18. Bonhoeffer, *op. cit.*, p. 219: " . . . we have to live in the world etsi deus non daretur."
19. Bonhoeffer, *op. cit.*, p. 219: "The God who is with us is the God who forsakes us."
20. Almost at the dawn of the Christian era, Ignatius had already written in his epistle to the Ephesians 8/2: "The carnal cannot live a spiritual life, nor can the spiritual live a carnal life, anymore than faith can act the part of infidelity, or infidelity the part of faith. But even the things you do in the flesh are spiritual, for you do all things in union with Jesus Christ." Calvin (*Institutes* III/2/24): "Unbelief is, in all men, always mixed with faith." On the other hand, Barth says: "There is certainly a justification for the doubter. But there is no justification for the doubt itself . . . no one should flirt with his unbelief or with his doubt. The theologian should only be sincerely *ashamed* of it" (*Evangelical Theology: an introduction*, New York, Holt, Rinehart and Winston, 1963, p. 131); in contrast to Paul Tillich, *Biblical Religion and the Search for Ultimate Reality* (Chicago, The University of Chicago Press, 1955), p. 85: "Faith comprises both itself and the doubt of itself." Cf. also Miguel de Unamuno, *The Agony of Christianity* (New York, Frederick Ungar Publishing Co., 1966). Even while

accepting doubt, faith need not consent to it: cf. *The Death of God,* pp. 12–13.

21. Barth, *The Word of God and the Word of Man* (New York, Harper Torchbooks, 1957), p. 324: " . . . the last thing, the ἔδχητοτ, the synthesis, is not the continuation, the result, the consequence, the next step after the next to the last, so to speak, *but,* on the contrary, is forever a radical break with everything next to the last; and this is just the secret of its connotation of Origin and its moving power."
22. *Summa Theologica* I, Qu. 2, Art. 1.
23. *Institutes* I/4/1; I/12. Cf. Bultmann, *Theology of the New Testament* II, p. 27.
24. Barth, *Church Dogmatics* 1/2 (Edinburgh, T. and T. Clark, 1957), ch. 17; Bultmann, *Theology of the New Testament* II, p. 27: "Right worship of God, that is, is an eschatological occurrence which God Himself brings about by His Spirit, and it becomes a reality by the coming of the Revealer." John 4/19–24.
25. Feuerbach, *The Essence of Christianity,* p. xxxvi.
26. Cf. Paul VI's Encyclical *Ecclesiam Suam.*

## III. No Other God

1. Ludwig Feuerbach, *The Essence of Christianity* (New York, Harper Torchbooks, 1957), p. 200: "The existence of God must therefore be in space—in general, a qualitative, sensational existence. But God is not seen, not heard, not perceived by the senses. He does not exist for me, if I do not exist for him; if I do not believe in a God, there is no God for me. If I am not devoutly disposed, if I do not raise myself above the life of the senses, he has no place in my consciousness. Thus he exists only insofar as he is felt, thought, believed in—the addition 'for me' is unnecessary. His existence therefore is a real one, yet at the same time not a real one; a spiritual existence, says the theologian."
2. Karl Barth, *The Word of God and the Word of Man* (New York, Harper Torchbooks, 1957), pp. 202–203.
3. "L'idole est dieu et n'est jamais tout-à-fait dieu" (Jacques Maritain, "Signe et symbole," *Revue Thomiste,* April 1938, p. 315).

4. Alexandre Vinet, *Etudes sur Blaise Pascal* (Paris, Librairie Fischbacher, 1904), p. 210.
5. *Pesikta derabbi Kahana,* p. 102 b. I owe this information to Professor Manfred Vogel.
6. Dietrich Bonhoeffer, *Letters and Papers from Prison* (New York, Macmillan Paperbacks, 1962), p. 219.
7. Bonhoeffer, *op. cit.*, p. 162.
8. Feuerbach, *op. cit.*, p. 32.
9. Ernst Cassirer, *An Essay on Man* (Garden City, New York, Anchor Books, 1956), pp. 98–99.
10. Vinet, *op. cit.*, p. 243.

## IV. The Word of God and the Word of Man

1. Herbert Braun, "The Problem of a New Testament Theology," *Journal for Theology and the Church* I, p. 181. *Cf.* Augustine's remarks on the differences between the LXX and the Hebrew text of the Old Testament in *The City of God* XVIII/43.
2. Daniel G. Hoffman, *Form and Fable in American Fiction* (New York, Oxford University Press, 1961), p. 174.
3. John Calvin, *Institutes* I/14/1; I/6/1.
4. Cf. Hans Urs von Balthasar, *Word and Revelation* (New York, Herder and Herder, 1964), p. 26.
5. Balthasar, *op. cit.*
6. Cf. Herbert Braun's similar statement about theonomy and autonomy in "The Problem of a New Testament Theology," *op. cit.*, p. 180; see also Karl Rahner, *Inspiration in the Bible* (New York, Herder and Herder, 1962), pp. 58–59.
7. Balthasar, *op. cit.*
8. Søren Kierkegaard, *The Sickness unto Death* (New York, Anchor Books, n.d.), p. 257.
9. Cf. Rahner, *op. cit.*
10. "Sic ite enim aurum per ferrum splendescit, sic sacra scriptura per saeculares disciplinas fulgescit." *Patr. Lat.*, CLVII, 1103A, quoted in Henri de Lubac, *Exégèse médiévale* I/1 (Paris, Aubier, 1959), p. 67.
11. Calvin, *Institutes,* I/7/3.
12. Heinrich Heppe, *Reformed Dogmatics* (London, Allen and Unwin, 1950), p. 31.

13. Reinhold Niebuhr, *Beyond Tragedy* (New York, Scribners, 1937), p. 28.
14. Alain, *Propos sur la religion* (Paris, Presses Universitaires de France, 1957, nouvelle édition), p. 21.
15. *Ibid.*, p. 15.
16. "La religion condamne la religion. Ce n'est pas l'école qui est sans Dieu, c'est l'Eglise qui est sans Dieu." *Ibid.*
17. Charles Baudelaire, *The Flowers of Evil,* ed. by Jackson and Marthiel Matthews (New York, New Directions, 1955), p. 10. This poem is translated by Richard Wilbur.
18. *Ibid.* p. xix.
19. Samuel Beckett, *Waiting for Godot,* translated from his original French text by the author (New York, Grove Press, 1956), p. 28.
20. Cf. Gabriel Vahanian, *Wait Without Idols* (New York, George Braziller, 1964), *passim;* "Christianity's Lost Iconoclasm," *The Nation,* Vol. 192, No. 16 (April 22, 1961).
21. T. S. Eliot, "The Rock," *Collected Poems* (New York, Harcourt, Brace and Co., 1958), p. 200.
22. *Ibid.*, p. 201.
23. *Ibid.*, p. 202.
24. Friedrich Nietzsche, "Den unbekannten Gott," in Schubert Ogden's selection and translation of *Existence and Faith* by Rudolf Bultmann (New York, Meridian Books, 1960), p. 28.
25. T. S. Eliot, *After Strange Gods: A Primer of Modern Heresy* (New York, Harcourt, Brace and Co., 1934), p. 30.
26. Rudolf Bultmann, *Primitive Christianity* (New York, Meridian Books, 1956), p. 17.
27. Gerhard Ebeling, *The Nature of Faith* (Philadelphia, Fortress Press, 1961), p. 90.
28. *Ibid.*, p. 87.
29. Brice Parain, *Recherches sur la nature et les fonctions du langage,* quoted by Paul Ricoeur, "Travail et Parole," *Esprit* 198 (Jan. 1953), p. 104.
30. *Loc. cit.*, p. 108.
31. *Ibid.*
32. Yves Berger, *Que peut la littérature?* (Paris, L'Inédit 10/18, 1965), p. 105.

33. William F. Lynch, S.J., *Christ and Apollo* (New York, Sheed and Ward, 1960), p. 15.
34. Cf. Numbers 12/6–8: "Hear my words: If there is a prophet among you, I the Lord make myself known to him in a vision, I speak with him in a dream. Not so with my servant Moses; he is entrusted with all my house. With him I speak mouth to mouth, clearly, and not in a dark speech; and he beholds the form of the Lord."
35. Rudolf Bultmann, "Revelation in the New Testament," *Existence and Faith* (New York, Meridian Books, 1960), p. 86.
36. Bultmann, *loc cit.*, p. 87.
37. Bultmann, *ibid.*
38. Bultmann, *loc. cit.*, p. 86.
39. Bultmann, *loc. cit.*, p. 70.
40. Ebeling, *op. cit.*, p. 105; cf. Isa. 52/1 sqq.; Heb. 4/12–13.
41. Ricoeur, *loc. cit.*, p. 112.
42. Bultmann, *loc. cit.*, pp. 72–73.
43. W. H. Auden, "The Dyer's Hand," *The Listener*, June 16, 1955.
44. In *Word and Faith* (English translation, Philadelphia, Fortress Press, 1963), Gerhard Ebeling speaks of the "wordliness of reality" (p. 351) or the world as a "word-event" (p. 412). G. Sohngen uses the phrase "verbal nature of the world"–*Gewortetsein der Welt*–in his book *Analogie und Metapher* (Munich, 1962) as quoted by L. Alonso Schockel in *The Inspired Word* (New York, Herder and Herder, 1965), p. 57.
45. Heidegger, "Hölderlin and the essence of poetry," *Existence and Being* (Chicago, Henry Regnery Company, 1949), p. 301.
46. Aristotle, *The Art of Poetry* (Translated by Ingram Bywater, Oxford, Clarendon Press, 1951), ch. 21; cf. Philip Wheelright, *Metaphor and Reality* (Bloomington, Indiana University Press, 1962), p. 72.
47. Cf. Reinhold Niebuhr, *An Interpretation of Christian Ethics* (New York, Harper and Brothers, 1935), p. 26.
48. Heidegger, *op. cit.*, p. 303.
49. While pointing out the dangers inherent in iconoclasm, by agreeing with C. G. Jung's description of Protestantism as

a history of continuous iconoclasm, nevertheless Paul Tillich fails, in my estimation, to identify faith as iconoclastic. This is due, I think, to a certain aestheticism which attaches to his understanding of the symbol. Cf. *The Protestant Era* (Chicago, The University of Chicago Press, 1948), p. xxiii. The same criticism applies to H. Westman's position as delineated in *The Springs of Creativity* (New York, Atheneum, 1961), pp. 14–15. For a definition of iconoclasm cf. *supra* and *Wait Without Idols* (New York, Braziller, 1964); Harvey Cox, *The Secular City* (New York, The Macmillan Company, 1965).

50. Saint-John Perse, *Winds* (New York, Pantheon Books, Inc., 1961), pp. 85–89.
51. Heidegger, *op. cit.*, p. 299.
52. Cf. Calvin, *Institutes* I/5/13.
53. Owen Barfield, *Saving the Appearances* (London, Faber and Faber, 1957), p. 75.
54. Cf. Chapter II, "The End of the Age of Religion?"
55. Bultmann, *loc. cit.*, p. 91.
56. Karl Barth, *The Word of God and the Word of Man* (New York, Harper Torchbooks, 1957), p. 216.

## V. Calvin: Theology and the Death of God

1. *Institutes* I/14/4 (The English translation is quoted from Calvin, *Institutes of the Christian Religion,* Vols. 21 and 22 of *The Library of Christian Classics,* edited by John T. McNeill and translated by Ford Lewis Battles, Philadelphia, Westminster Press, 1960).
2. *Institutes* III/2/14.
3. *Institutes* III/2/7.
4. *Institutes* I/2/1.
5. *Institutes* I/2/1.
6. François Wendel, *Calvin: Sources et évolution de sa pensée religieuse* (Paris, Presses Universitaires de France, 1950), p. v (my translation).
7. Karl Jaspers.
8. From a sermon on Deuteronomy (4/39–43), *Opera Calvini* XXVI, *Corpus Reformatorum* LIV (Brunsvigae, C. A. Schwetschke et filium, 1883), col. 224 (my trans-

lation); cf. Jean Boisset, *Sagesse et Sainteté dans la pensée de Calvin* (Paris, Presses Universitaires de France, 1959), p. 184.

9. *Institutes* I/1/1.
10. *Institutes* I/1/1.
11. *Institutes* I/13/1; cf. F. Wendel, *op. cit.*, p. 113.
12. *Institutes* I/2/2.
13. *Institutes* I/13/2; 1/13/10; Heb. 1/3: "Splendor et figura substantiae ejus."
14. *Institutes* I/3/1.
15. *Institutes* I/3/1.
16. *Institutes* I/13/1.
17. Wilhelm Niesel, *The Theology of Calvin* (Philadelphia, Westminster Press, 1965), p. 60; *Institutes* 1/13/2: "But God also designates himself by another special mark to distinguish himself more precisely from idols."
18. Alluding to Ps. 44/3 Calvin calls the "land" a "symbol" of man's adoption by God, and even uses in the 1560 French edition of the *Institutes* (III/21/5) the word *méreau,* a token with which one was entitled to participate in the Lord's Supper.
19. *Institutes* I/13/7.
20. *Institutes* III/1/4.
21. *Institutes* I/13/13.
22. Thomas Aquinas, *Summa Theologiae* I, Qu. 23, Art. 1, 2.
23. *Ibid.* I, Qu. 23, Art. 2.
24. Calvin, *The Eternal Predestination of God,* p. 110; cf. also *Institutes* II/24/5; III/22/1.
25. *Institutes* III/23/12; III/23/1.
26. *Institutes* III/21/5; III/22/1.
27. *Institutes* III/23/12; cf. also G. Deluz, *Prédestination et liberté* (Neuchâtel, Delachaux et Niestlé, 1942), p. 97.
28. Calvin, *The Secret Providence of God,* p. 262.
29. *Ibid.*, p. 261.
30. Cf. *Consensus Genevensis:* "Should anyone wish to understand this in a more pregnant way: election, though it precedes faith, can only be grasped through (in) faith." Cf. also Wilhelm Pauck, *The Heritage of the Reformation* (Glencoe, Ill., The Free Press, and Boston, Beacon Press, 1950), pp. 62–63.

31. For much of this part I am indebted to the teachings of Pierre Maury.
32. *Institutes* III/21/1.
33. *Institutes* III/10/6.
34. *Institutes* I/5/1.
35. *Institutes* II/1/11; cf. also III/2/25.
36. Sermon LXXVII on Deuteronomy, *Opera Calvini* XXVII, col. 110 (my translation).
37. William Faulkner, "Black Music," *Collected Stories of William Faulkner* (New York, Random House, 1950), p. 809; cf. also Franz Kafka, "Reflections," *The Great Wall of China* (New York, Schocken Books, 1946), p. 307.
38. *Institutes* III/2/4.
39. *Institutes* III/7/1.
40. To wit, for example, his hesitations about indiscriminately appropriating the traditional trinitarian terminology (*Institutes* I/13/3–6).

## VI. The Church, the World, and Ethics

1. Cf. Harvey Cox, "Sociology of Religion in a Post-Religious Era," *The Christian Scholar* XLVIII (1965), No. 1.
2. Paul Lehman, *Ethics in a Christian Context* (New York, Harper and Row, 1963).
3. Joseph Fletcher, *Situation Ethics* (Philadelphia, Westminster Press, 1966); John A. T. Robinson, *Christian Morals Today* (Philadelphia, Westminster Press, 1964).
4. Paul Ramsey, *Basic Christian Ethics* (New York, Scribners, 1950); *Deeds and Rules in Christian Ethics* (Scottish Journal of Theology Occasional Papers No. 11, London and Edinburgh, Oliver and Boyd, 1965).
5. *Cum grano salis*, to be sure.